Karl Popper

Series Introduction

The *Major Conservative and Libertarian Thinkers* series aims to show that there is a rigorous, scholarly tradition of social and political thought that may be broadly described as 'conservative', 'libertarian' or some combination of the two.

The series aims to show that conservatism is not simply a reaction against contemporary events, nor a privileging of intuitive thought over deductive reasoning; libertarianism is not simply an apology for unfettered capitalism or an attempt to justify a misguided atomistic concept of the individual. Rather, the thinkers in this series have developed coherent intellectual positions that are grounded in empirical reality and also founded upon serious philosophical reflection on the relationship between the individual and society, how the social institutions necessary for a free society are to be established and maintained, and the implications of the limits to human knowledge and certainty.

Each volume in the series presents a thinker's ideas in an accessible and cogent manner to provide an indispensable work for students with varying degrees of familiarity with the topic as well as more advanced scholars.

The following twenty volumes that make up the entire *Major Conservative and Libertarian Thinkers* series are written by international scholars and experts:

The Salamanca School by Andre Azevedo Alves (LSE, UK) and
    José Manuel Moreira (Universidade de Aveiro, Portugal)
Thomas Hobbes by R. E. R. Bunce (Cambridge, UK)
John Locke by Eric Mack (Tulane, UK)
David Hume by Christopher J. Berry (Glasgow, UK)
Adam Smith by James Otteson (Yeshiva, US)
Edmund Burke by Dennis O'Keeffe (Buckingham, UK)
Alexis de Tocqueville by Alan S Kahan (Paris, France)
Herbert Spencer by Alberto Mingardi (Istituto Bruno Leoni, Italy)

Ludwig von Mises by Richard Ebeling (Northwood, US)
Joseph A. Schumpeter by John Medearis (Riverside, California, US)
F. A. Hayek by Adam Tebble (UCL, UK)
Michael Oakeshott by Edmund Neill (Oxford, UK)
Karl Popper by Phil Parvin (Loughborough, UK)
Ayn Rand by Mimi Gladstein (Texas, US)
Milton Friedman by William Ruger (Texas State, US)
Russell Kirk by John Pafford (Northwood, US)
James M. Buchanan by John Meadowcroft (King's College London, UK)
The Modern Papacy by Samuel Gregg (Acton Institute, US)
Murray Rothbard by Gerard Casey (UCD, Ireland)
Robert Nozick by Ralf Bader (St Andrews, UK)

Of course, in any series of this nature, choices have to be made as to which thinkers to include and which to leave out. Two of the thinkers in the series – F. A. Hayek and James M. Buchanan – have written explicit statements rejecting the label 'conservative'. Similarly, other thinkers, such as David Hume and Karl Popper, may be more accurately described as classical liberals than either conservatives or libertarians. But these thinkers have been included because a full appreciation of this particular tradition of thought would be impossible without their inclusion; conservative and libertarian thought cannot be fully understood without some knowledge of the intellectual contributions of Hume, Hayek, Popper and Buchanan, among others. While no list of conservative and libertarian thinkers can be perfect, then, it is hoped that the volumes in this series come as close as possible to providing a comprehensive account of the key contributors to this particular tradition.

John Meadowcroft
King's College London

Karl Popper

Phil Parvin

Major Conservative and Libertarian Thinkers

Series Editor: John Meadowcroft

B L O O M S B U R Y

NEW YORK • LONDON • NEW DELHI • SYDNEY

Bloomsbury Academic
An imprint of Bloomsbury Publishing Plc

1385 Broadway   50 Bedford Square
New York   London
NY 10018   WC1B 3DP
USA   UK

www.bloomsbury.com

Hardback edition first published in 2010 by the
Continuum International Publishing Group Inc.

This paperback edition published by Bloomsbury Academic 2013

© Phil Parvin, 2013

Library of Congress Cataloging-in-Publication Data
A catalog record for this title is available from the Library of Congress

ISBN: HB: 978-0-8264-3222-3
PB: 978-1-4411-8539-6
ePub: 978-1-6235-6733-0

Typeset by Newgen Imaging Systems Pvt Ltd, Chennai, India
Printed and bound in the United States of America

Contents

Series Editor's Preface

Karl Popper was one of the most important and controversial thinkers of the twentieth century. Today he is best known for his contributions to the philosophy of science and the history of ideas. In the former Popper argued that only scientific theories that could be subject to falsification could make a contribution to knowledge; propositions that could not be falsified could not advance human understanding of the world. In the latter Popper traced the origins of twentieth-century totalitarianism to the ideas of Plato and Hegel whom he believed had provided the intellectual foundations for communist, fascist and Nazi regimes that subjugated the rights of individuals to the pursuit of collective ends.

There were elements of Popper's thought, then, that were clearly libertarian or conservative in character: Popper embraced individual freedom and adopted a methodological individualist approach to his scholarly work; he believed in a dynamic, cosmopolitan 'open society' characterized by free thought and expression and contrasted this ideal with the 'closed society' that was organized to facilitate the collective pursuit of a social end determined by political elites; and he was sceptical of radical change that aimed to enact a pre-determined blueprint for the organization of society.

In other respects, however, Popper's thought does not fit so easily into the libertarian or conservative tradition. Popper's politics were recognizably social democratic: he believed in incremental social reform aimed at improving the lot of the poorest in society and was at ease with the Western European post-war welfare state; he believed the scope of the market should be limited, and had faith in the power of public reason emerging from democratic deliberation to guide the state in the effective amelioration of social problems. Popper's open society, then, was not a free market utopia, but a political community in which diverse people engaged with one another in constructive dialogue to seek political solutions to common problems.

As Phil Parvin of the University of Loughborough shows in this masterly account of Popper's work, Popper made important and enduring contributions to the libertarian and conservative traditions, but it would be a mistake to uncritically label him a conservative or libertarian. Rather, Popper was a scholar who contributed to a range of different fields without being shackled to one particular perspective or approach. It is in this context that we should understand Popper's contribution to libertarian and conservative thought.

This volume contributes to the *Major Conservative and Libertarian Thinkers* series by presenting Popper's thought in an accessible and cogent form. It is an outstanding work that provides a thorough account of Popper's life and work, considers the reception of Popper's work by his contemporaries, and then shows Popper's continuing relevance, in particular to twenty-first century Anglo-American political philosophy. This book will prove indispensable to those unfamiliar with Popper's ideas as well as more advanced scholars.

John Meadowcroft
King's College London

Acknowledgments

This book was completed during the first year of my Leverhulme Early Career Fellowship at the University of Cambridge. I should like to thank the Leverhulme Trust for funding this and other research, and my colleagues in the Department of Politics and International Studies for being such supportive and welcoming hosts. In particular, I should like to thank Andrew Gamble, Helen Thompson, and David Runciman who together went to a lot of trouble in supporting my application to Leverhulme, and have remained valued colleagues ever since. I should also like to thank the Master, Fellows, and Staff of Trinity Hall, who have provided a wonderful environment in which to develop my ideas, and everyone at the Center for British Studies at the University of California, Berkeley, at which I was a Visiting Scholar for the Fall semester, 2009.

A number of friends and colleagues provided helpful comments on earlier portions of the book. In particular, Mark Bevir provided invaluable advice and help, Melissa Lane directed me toward a number of important texts, and David Owen helped me straighten out a number of confusions I had about the history of analytical philosophy. Special thanks should go to Duncan Bell and Ben Jackson, both of whom read and commented upon the entire draft. The book is much better for their input, but would no doubt be even better had I had the space to incorporate all their great suggestions. In the writing of this book, I drew inspiration from many texts and authors. Malachi Hacohen's *Karl Popper: The Formative Years, 1902–1945: Politics and Philosophy in Interwar Vienna* was particularly helpful, especially with regard to Popper's early life and career. Thanks are also due to John Meadowcroft, and Continuum, for asking me to write this book.

Finally, I should like to thank Clare Chambers, who has provided incredible help and support for this and many other projects, and Harley, who, in the very best way possible, has convinced me of the futility of long-term planning.

1

Intellectual Biography

Karl Popper was on one of the most important philosophers of the twentieth century. His influence can be seen across many disciplines, and he wrote widely on subjects as diverse and complex as the philosophy of science and mathematics, music, history, psychology, politics, logic, and epistemology. He was not strictly a political philosopher, although his famous defence of individual liberty against the purported totalitarian tendencies of thinkers like Plato, Marx, and Hegel continues to represent an important contribution to Western political thought. His critique of historicism as an approach to understanding not only philosophy, society and politics, but music, science, and history itself has had an enormous and lasting effect on the conduct of debates in these areas. His approach to the appropriate conduct of the natural and social sciences still represents one of the most important contributions to epistemology and the philosophy of science made in the twentieth century. His application of this approach to all aspects of human inquiry, including politics, provided a new and provocative approach to understanding not merely politics and society, but the appropriate ends of philosophy.

Despite all this, Popper nevertheless remains a marginal figure in the history of political thought. Contemporary political theorists rarely engage with his ideas, and even more rarely encourage their students to study him.

Popper was controversial. *The Open Society and Its Enemies* and *The Poverty of Historicism*, his two most famous contributions to

social and political theory, caused outrage among many philosophers, and derision among others. His books were criticized for
lacking in scholarship, for denigrating the name of some of the
most revered thinkers in the history of Western civilization,
and for defending the simplistic liberal democratic bourgeois
hegemony against more radical visions of society and politics.
Popper's political thought was driven by a profound philosophical rationalism which was at odds with a lot of political philosophy of the time, and a belief in the need for social and
political theory to be of *practical* help to legislators and policy-
makers which ran (and still runs) counter to the ideal theorizing
popular among many analytical political philosophers, and the
abstractionism of many postmodernists and poststructuralists.
But it was also driven by a deep and clear moral sense. *The Open
Society*, written during World War II when Europe seemed on
the brink of falling to fascism, represents nothing less than a
philosophical defence of Western civilization and the values
upon which it was founded. It represents a vindication of the
values of freedom, equality, and democracy, and a withering,
visceral attack upon those who would deny these values in the
name of national unity, or stability, or the good of all. Popper's
language is often brutal, his arguments unmeasured by scholarly
convention, and his attacks personal and devastating. His commitment to the open society was trenchant and unwavering,
and his hatred for those throughout history whom he thought
provided the Nazis, the Fascists and (later) the Communists
with the philosophical tools to justify their evil, was obvious.
Small wonder, then, that his work caused such controversy when
it emerged, and why so many current philosophers are unsure as
to what to do with it. His political prescriptions cannot be easily
associated with any political ideology, although thinkers from all
points on the political spectrum have tried to claim him for their
own. And his epistemological views place him outside many of
the dominant approaches to understanding society and politics.
Popper's was an original, controversial, flawed, but important
contribution to political thought which has stood the test of

time, but which remains all but ignored by social and political theorists. In what follows, we will come to see more clearly what Popper had to say about politics, society, and philosophy, the controversy he caused, and the enduring implications his claims have for the contemporary study of society and its problems.

Early beginnings

Karl Popper's story begins in Vienna towards the tail-end of the Habsburg Empire. At that time, the city was the capital of a huge multi-ethnic empire, and nationalism was becoming an increasingly visible and important force in Austrian politics. Between 1867 and 1879 Austrian liberalism achieved a great many positive social and political reforms, including economic modernization and the expansion of public education, which would profoundly shape the social and political environment into which Karl Popper would later be born. But it also left a darker legacy that would come to dominate Popper's world. Austrian liberalism had an assimilationist and nationalist character: full citizenship was limited to those who 'exhibited the solid character of the German *Burger*' (Hacohen, 2000; 32). Vienna was, at that time, the 'most assimilated city in Europe' (Edmonds & Eidenow, 2002; 72). The city 'had the highest conversion rate of Jews to Christianity of any European urban centre', partly due to the pervasive anti-Semitism felt by many Jews (Edmonds & Eidenow, 2002; 72). As time went on, Austrian liberalism collapsed into German nationalism, as liberals sought to unify an increasingly fragmented middle class under a new and visceral political vision rooted in ethnicity. This vision became increasingly powerful, and increasingly detrimental to the lives and interests of Jews like Karl's parents, Simon and Jenny – especially Jewish immigrants like his father (Jenny Popper had been born in Vienna). Like so many other Jewish families living in the city, the Poppers renounced their membership of the Jewish community and converted to Lutheranism in 1900 but despite doing so, and despite adopting the work ethic and values of German *Kultur*, the Poppers – like most Jews – were never truly welcomed into mainstream society. The early liberal idea that one might acquire the qualities of 'the good citizen' through acculturation and hard work appeared to have been replaced by a newer appeal to ethnicity and race. Consequently, the Jews kept themselves to themselves, living, working, socializing, and marrying within a broadly cohesive and generally exclusive and excluded community.

Vienna at that time was also home to a radical progressive movement and the Poppers moved in the same circles as many of its most important members. Even before Popper's birth, radical progressives had 'rebelled against the social conservatism of mainstream liberalism and sought an opening for the workers. They opted for a bourgeois – proletarian alliance under the auspices of an enlightened bureaucracy that would promote social legislation, economic modernization, and scientific education' (Hacohen, 2000; 24). They sought a new leftist agenda, as a challenge to Austrian liberalism. They believed in the capacity of science and 'social technology' to resolve the problems of poverty and the unequal distribution of resources among the rich and the poor, and believed, therefore, that social justice required a scientific understanding of these problems (and their solutions). They established the Vienna Fabian Society in 1891, and the *Sozialpolitische partei* in 1896, and used these and other fora to campaign for universal male suffrage and welfare reforms and against Catholicism and anti-Semitism.

So it was that on 28 July 1902, Karl Popper was born into an imperial city divided along political, social, economic, and religious lines, into a newly Christian household, to parents who had given up their religion and embraced the dominant culture in order to succeed, but who were nevertheless considered with suspicion by the largely anti-Semitic majority. Nevertheless, Popper's parents had succeeded in climbing to the upper echelons of Viennese society. Simon Popper was a highly-paid lawyer who, together with his wife, two daughters and new son, lived in a huge 20-room apartment which provided enough space to house his family, his many books, secretary's and servants' quarters, as well as offices for the various charitable organizations that he ran. In his *Autobiography*, Popper described his father as 'more of a scholar than a lawyer', with interests in poetry, history, and philosophy. His book collection, so large that it spilled from his library and into the rest of the apartment, apparently contained around 14,000 works, including those of Plato, Bacon, Descartes, Spinoza, Nietzsche, Locke, Kant, and Mill, as well as the 'standard authors of German, French, English, Russian, and Scandinavian literature' (Popper 1974/2002; 6); it included a large history collection, classical works, contemporary philosophy and literature, and recent Viennese publications on politics, social reform, and psychoanalysis, as well as the works of Charles Darwin.

Popper's immediate family, as well as those members of the progressive movement which his parents were a part of, encouraged in him an early appreciation of knowledge, scholarship, and culture. He described himself as a 'bookish' child, 'rather priggish' and a 'softy'. From a very young age, young Karl was fascinated by philosophical issues, and his inquiry into these issues was encouraged. He wrote that, at the age of 8, he became much exercised by the nature of infinity, and at 12 or 13 he was enquiring as to 'the problems of the origin of life, left open by Darwin, and whether life is simply a chemical process' (Popper, 1974/2002; 12). And he claimed that it was at the age of 15 that he stumbled across an idea that would later inform his most important mature philosophy: the 'problem of essentialism'.

Popper described his school life as 'boring in the extreme'. Despite his teachers' best efforts, he found his lessons to be nothing but 'hours and hours of torture' and a 'waste of time'. Born into a family and a social milieu which valued critique and engagement with conventional wisdom, Popper hated the way teachers attempted to 'drill' knowledge into their students. He sought a more reflective and interactive way of learning, one which would allow students to develop their critical faculties, rather than accept what they were told uncritically. This view would become strengthened in the years during and after World War I, as he himself came to challenge many of the views he had held up to that time.

He was 12 when the war broke out. He recalled the day well. A socialist family friend Athur Arndt often took him to meetings of the Monists, an association of progressive socialists dedicated to the 'scientific reform of philosophy, education, and the law', where the young Karl would learn about the progressive cause and discuss political reform (Hacohen, 2000; 42). Popper was on a hike with the Monists when he first heard the news that Archduke Franz Ferdinand had been assassinated; war was declared one week later, on his birthday. The war was to have a profound and irrevocable effect both on the Austro-Hungarian empire and Popper. The social, political, and economic divisions which predated the war (between the rich and the poor, the Jewish minority and the Christian majority, the liberals and the progressives) were exacerbated and politicized. As a consequence, Viennese society became much more fragmented and reactionary. As the war started to go badly, immigrants (many of whom were Jews) flooded into Austria. Anti-Semitism rose, and Jewish refugees were viewed by many as parasites. Severe food and fuel shortages increased social tensions, culminating in strikes and demonstrations. Social and economic chaos, coupled with huge and devastating losses from the Front, conspired to make the situation untenable. By the time the Armistice was signed in October 1918 (marking the end of the Habsburg empire) Viennese society had altered radically.

Young people at this time were becoming increasingly politicized, and Karl Popper was no exception. At around the same time that Popper was rebelling against the authority embodied in the Austrian school system he was rebelling too against those ideas which dominated political discourse at the time. In 1918, Popper left school (against the wishes of his parents) and enrolled as an unmatriculated student at the University of Vienna. He also became involved in student and youth politics and embraced communism as a means to end the conflict, poverty, and prevailing social unrest. This sympathy for communism would prove short-lived, however, and would be extinguished in 1919 at a student demonstration organized by communists like himself at which a number of students were shot and killed by the police. In *Unended Quest*, he wrote of being 'shocked by the brutality of the police, but also by myself. For I felt that, as a Marxist, I bore part of the responsibility – at least in principle. Marxist theory demands that the class struggle be intensified in order to speed up the coming of socialism. Its thesis is that although the revolution may claim some victims, capitalism is claiming more victims than the whole socialist revolution' (Popper, 1974/2002; 33). The shootings took place a few days before Popper's 17th birthday and he claimed that by the time he was 17 he had become an anti-Marxist. 'I realized the dogmatic character of the creed and its incredible intellectual arrogance,' he wrote. 'It was a terrible thing to arrogate oneself to a kind of knowledge which made it a duty to risk the lives of other people for an uncritically accepted dogma, or for a dream which might turn out not to be realizable. It was particularly depressing for an intellectual who could read and think. It was awfully depressing to have fallen into such a trap.' (Popper, 1974/2002; 34). Popper was particularly 'revolted' by the 'intellectual presumption of some of [his] Marxist friends and fellow students, who almost took it for granted that they were the future leaders of the working class'. They had, he said, 'no special intellectual qualifications. All they could claim was some acquaintance with Marxist literature – though not even a thorough one, and certainly not a critical one.' (Popper, 1974/2002; 35).

We can, perhaps, glimpse in these statements echoes of what was to come. In *Unended Quest* Popper praised the workers of Vienna and their political movement, while at the same time rejecting the 'historicist ideas of their social democratic leaders as fatally mistaken' (Popper, 1974/2002; 35). Their leaders were able to inspire in them a sense that they were embarked upon a mission no less important than the liberation of mankind from poverty, from hunger, and from oppression. It was a movement premised on the education of the workers – the provision of those intellectual resources necessary for individuals to 'emancipate themselves and thus to liberate mankind' (Hacohen, 2000; 36). The progressive aim of establishing education as something that all people should have access to (regardless of whether they are rich or poor) stayed with Popper, who advocated the state provision of education for all in *The Open Society*. The idea, therefore, that freedom and equality could be secured by state institutions which provided people with the ability to take their lives (and their political destinies) into their own hands lived on in his later work and formed an important theme in his critiques of totalitarianism and fascism, and the historicist doctrines on which he believed they were built. Self-emancipation through knowledge, social reform through human agency, a hatred of poverty, injustice and oppression: Popper's view was that it was possible to hold all these ideas while rejecting Marxism.

The Pedagogic Institute

Perhaps as a reaction to the self-importance and lofty arrogance of his Marxist 'comrades', Popper sought his own solutions to social problems, while also seeking a practical and professional career that would have seemed somewhat alien to his intellectual friends. In 1922, at the age of 20, Popper passed his *matura* (a school-leaving exam), allowing him to become a fully matriculated student at the University. Two years later, he passed a second *matura* from a teacher-training college. This was at the same time as he was also learning to become a cabinet maker, as a carpenter's apprentice. At that time, teaching posts were rare and carpentry did not agree with him, and so he changed jobs, and spent some time as a social worker for neglected children. Popper appeared to be drifting. The social, political, and economic upheavals of the war and the revolution destroyed old certainties and created an environment in which settled patterns of life were disrupted. This emerging sense of uncertainty was reflected in the intellectual and artistic movements of the time. With the dissolution of established traditions in the wake of social and political conflict, Vienna became the

> city of Ernst Mach and the theory of the fluctuating and uncertain self; of Freud and the power of the unconscious; of Schoenberg and the ousting of conventional tonality in favour of the twelve tone system. Here within a single period were Arthur Schnitzler's literature on the interior monologue and of the sexual drive as the prime mover of human relationships; Adolf Loos and the stripping away of ornament for ornament's sake in architecture; . . . and Karl Kraus and his attack on linguistic forms – clichés, metaphors – that disguised realities in politics and culture. (Edmonds & Eidenow, 2002, 76)

The new and uncertain social order provided Popper with a developing political sense of what he thought needed to be done to rebuild society along more humane and just lines, but precious little guidance as to what he should *do* with his life. Meanwhile, his interest in politics and philosophy endured and intensified. He fell under the influence of Karl Polanyi, a respected social theorist who argued for a non-Marxist form of socialism, and Leonard Nelson, a radical Kantian philosopher and cosmopolitan who argued for the establishment of an international legal system and the adoption of a 'Socratic method' in teaching the young. Together, Polanyi and Nelson had a profound effect on Popper; Polanyi showed that a commitment to social justice was not incompatible with bourgeois economics (and hence, that socialism need not be revolutionary, or aim at the socialization of the workforce), and Nelson's work on Kant, and his conception of a 'critical philosophy' which held Socrates and Kant as exemplars of reasoned philosophical inquiry (who were betrayed by the likes of Hegel, Fichte, and Schelling), provided crucial elements to Popper's developing philosophy of knowledge and politics, and provided new insights into the relationship between freedom and egalitarianism.

In 1925 the City of Vienna established the Pedagogic Institute – an autonomous institution linked to the University, aimed at encouraging reform of the primary and secondary school system. Popper was one of several social workers who were admitted to the Institute. He described his years there as ones devoted to studying, reading, teaching, and writing, but not publishing. He taught classes in psychology and, through doing so, met Karl Buhler, Professor of Psychology at the University. In his second year, he met Heinrich Gomperz, Professor of Philosophy at the University, whose work on epistemology would greatly influence him, and Julius Kraft, with whom he shared a non-Marxist understanding of socialism and with whom he often discussed the failings of Marx. It was also at the Institute that Popper would meet Josephine Henniger, whom he would later marry.

It was at the Pedagogic Institute that Popper first became interested in psychology and epistemology. Through conversations with Buhler, Gomperz and Kraft, Popper was able to develop his earlier general concerns about the way in which children were being taught in Vienna at that time. He became increasingly consumed by questions about how individuals acquire knowledge of the world, what form this knowledge took, and what limits there might be to obtaining it. His 1927 thesis 'Habit and the Experience of Lawfulness' – submitted in order to complete his two years at the Institute – explored the relationship between logic and psychology, focusing primarily on the ways in which children acquire knowledge. He argued that children are naturally conservative in that they prefer order to disorder. Consequently, he believed, children try as far as possible to impose order on the world by understanding it in terms of regularities. This idea – that human beings seek to impose regularity on their lives and upon the world in which they live by deriving overarching laws (of nature, of history, of tradition, of nation) – later assumed a pivotal place in Popper's mature political philosophy. Popper conceived the thesis as a 'Kantian critique of the limits of scientific pedagogy', and he used it to criticize many of the trends in educational reform that were dominant at the time (and which the Institute had been established to encourage). The result was a paper which questioned the idea that children could be educated into becoming critical thinkers, and which sought to provide a general description of the process by which children acquired knowledge by appealing to the standard inductive method of scientific inquiry, rather than psychology. Popper extended these themes in his PhD thesis which he submitted a year later. The thesis, entitled 'On the Methodological Problem of Cognitive Psychology' sought to resolve 'the problem of the boundaries among psychology, logic, and epistemology' by providing some criterion of 'demarcation' between epistemology and psychology (Hacohen, 2000; 63). Popper claimed that he was unhappy with his thesis, and described it in his autobiography as 'a kind of hasty last minute affair' (Popper, 1974/2002; 87). Nevertheless, his examiners (Karl Buhler, and Moritz Schlick) passed it with distinction. Whether Popper was happy with it or not, the thesis marks Popper's break with psychology and his turn towards logic and science. Popper's PhD represented an argument against psychologism (the idea that all knowledge can be understood in terms of subjective thought processes), and a development of the claim (made by Buhler) that 'we do not think in images but in terms of problems and their tentative solutions' (Popper, 1974/2002; 86). This claim – that human beings are principally problem solvers – reappears in Popper's later work, including *The Poverty of Historicism* and *The Open Society*. The turn to science was more or less completed a year later when, in 1929, at the age of 26, Popper qualified to teach mathematics and physical sciences at secondary school level. His thesis (submitted in order to graduate) was on the history and foundations of geometry, and included some of his earliest thoughts on scientific rationality and progress.

Wittgenstein and the Vienna Circle

Despite not being a member of the academy, Popper continued to move among some of the most talented academics in Europe, especially in the fields of epistemology, science, and mathematics. Interwar Vienna was home to a lively and intense intellectual community of scholars from many different disciplines, both within the academy and beyond it. Even before the outbreak of the World War I, Vienna had always been known for its literary, academic, and cultural life found in the coffee shops and meeting places along the *Ringstrasse*. Intellectuals and activists would meet and argue and, over 'a coffee, a glass of water and perhaps a strudel, an article would be written, an argument renewed, a play reviewed, an introduction made' (Edmonds & Eidenow, 2002; 58). Popper was always sceptical – if not contemptuous – of this intellectual scene, viewing it as a self-indulgence among the affluent, and dominated by passing intellectual fads and fashions. Popper once remarked that Wittgenstein's *Tractatus* (which he loathed) 'smelled of the coffee house'.

Popper may not have been a regular at the coffee houses of Vienna, but he was greatly influenced by other academic gatherings, especially in the years during and immediately after the submission of his PhD. Heinrich Gomperz, for example, ran an informal discussion group on the history of ideas, in which academics from a range of disciplines would discuss historical and philosophical issues. Through Gomperz, Popper was invited to attend these meetings and, in fact, it was perhaps his performance at one such meeting that kept him from becoming a member of the more important and influential Vienna Circle, convened by his PhD examiner Moritz Schlick. Schlick – who also attended Gomperz's discussion group from time to time – had never been a great admirer of Popper (the fact that he passed Popper's PhD thesis with distinction was apparently more to do with his respect for Buhler than Popper's work). When Popper used the session to viciously attack Ludwig Wittgenstein – one of Schlick's heroes and the intellectual father of the Vienna Circle – Schlick left halfway through in disgust and denounced Popper's critique as a caricature. Whether that moment was decisive or not, no invitation was made to Popper to join the Circle.

Popper appeared to revel in his exclusion from the Vienna Circle, and was always proud of the fact that he was never welcomed as a member. Otto Neurath, a member of the Circle, once described Popper as the group's 'official opposition', a role that Popper relished. Popper would spend most of his career attacking the philosophical foundations of the Circle, and developing arguments against many of its most influential members. And influential they were. The Vienna Circle, established by Schlick was one of the most important academic groups in interwar Europe. Regular members of the group – which drew leading thinkers in the fields of philosophy, logic, mathematics, the social sciences, and the natural and physical sciences – included such luminaries as Rudolph Carnap, Otto Neurath, Hans Hahn, Kurt Godel, Friedrich Waissman, and Herbert Feigl. Often joined by international visitors like V. W. O. Quine from America, A. J. Ayer from Britain, Alfred Tarski from Poland, and Carl Hempel from Berlin, the meetings of the Circle were a veritable who's who of philosophical and scientific talent. The raison d'etre of the Circle, and the ideology which bound this eclectic group of thinkers together, was the idea that the methods of the physical sciences should be applied to philosophy. Their stance was most obviously opposed to German Idealism – embodied in the work of Hegel, Fichte, Schelling, and Kant – which held that there were things about the world which could not be known through observation and that, consequently, the scientific method could not yield true or complete knowledge about the world. The German Idealists thus held that philosophy and science were separate endeavours, that there were genuine questions which could not be answered by science (like questions of metaphysics, ontology, ethics, and theology), and that philosophy was uniquely suited to resolving these issues. The members of the Vienna Circle, on the other hand, believed that philosophy should learn from science, and that philosophy would always be subordinate to science as the means by which knowledge about the world might be meaningfully pursued and acquired. Their principal aim, therefore, was to demarcate 'physics' (that is, what could be known scientifically) from 'metaphysics' (which could not). The criterion of demarcation was drawn from Wittgenstein's *Tractatus Logico Philosophicus* (1921), which became the Circle's bible.

In the *Tractatus*, Wittgenstein explored the relationship between language and reality and argued that this relationship was a *descriptive* one: the world is the totality of facts which exist around us, and we use language to *describe* this world. There are, therefore, two ways in which a statement might be said to be meaningful: it must either be verifiable through observation (in the sense that it meaningfully describes something that can be seen or experienced in the world), or 'analytical' in the sense that its meaning is derived entirely from the logical relationship of the particular words used. Statements or utterances which do not intelligibly describe some fact in the world, and which are also not logical statements which derive their meaning from the internal structure of the statement itself, are *meaningless*. For example, the statement 'a rectangle has four sides' is *analytical* (and, hence, meaningful) in the sense that its meaning is derived from the words used in that order, not because it necessarily tells us something *true* about the world. It is a tautology: its meaning is derived from the logic of the statement itself. Similarly, a statement such as 'that shoebox is rectangular' is meaningful in the sense that it can be verified through observation and experience. However, a statement such as 'God made that shoebox' is neither analytical not verifiable, and hence, is meaningless.

Philosophy, then, for Wittgenstein (and the Vienna Circle), was not the search for truth but the search for meaning: the search for statements about the world which were either logically meaningful in their own right or gained their meaning through verification. Consequently, metaphysical statements such as 'The mind and body are distinct' or 'God is the prime mover of the Universe' were considered meaningless. They are not 'untrue' or 'wrong', they are merely beyond the scope of philosophy to resolve. While *science* determines what is true, *philosophy* should concern itself with determining the meaning of words, and of the utterances that they compose. This approach was named 'logical positivism', and it embodied a radical approach to understanding the purposes and limits of philosophy. For if the principal criteria of demarcation between the meaningfulness and non-meaningfulness of statements was whether they could be verified through an observation of the real world, or whether they were meaningful in terms of their own internal logic, then it was not merely *metaphysical* statements which were consigned to the rubbish bin but all statements which fail the verification test, such as those of aesthetics, ethics, politics, and theology. Claims such as 'Beethoven was a better composer than Mozart', or 'All human beings should live virtuous lives', or 'God gave human beings rights' are meaningless, because none of these claims are analytical (in Wittgenstein's sense) or empirically verifiable. Thus, the Vienna Circle believed that Wittgenstein's philosophy of language had laid bare the real content and aims of philosophy, and provided the criteria by which one might determine which questions or statements were important and legitimate, and which were meaningless and redundant.

Popper agreed with the broad claim made by the logical positivists that science and philosophy might complement one another. After all, he shared the logical positivists' commitment to rationality, reason, and intellectual inquiry, and believed that it was important to distinguish between real knowledge and subjective opinion. He was, for example, supportive of Carnap's pleas for 'rationality, [and] for greater intellectual responsibility'. Carnap, he said, 'asks us to learn from the way in which mathematicians and scientists proceed, and he contrasts this with the depressing ways of philosophers: their pretentious wisdom, and their arrogation of knowledge which they present to us with a minimum of rational, or critical, argument' (Popper,

1974/2002; 100). Again, we can sense Popper's disdain for the philosophers in their coffee houses, so many of whom felt they could pontificate on the nature of reality without having to trouble themselves with providing evidence for their claims. The logical positivists' attitude was 'the attitude of the enlightenment', and Popper claimed to feel very much at one with the Vienna Circle's claim that philosophers (like anyone else) should limit themselves to what can be established through reason and rational argument, and that one should be sceptical of bold assertions of philosophical truth that could not be criticized rationally.

But Popper was not a logical positivist, and was not a member of the Vienna Circle, even though many believed that he was. Indeed, he was keen to disassociate himself from the Circle. Popper rejected the creed of the logical positivists because their aim was to debunk metaphysics, aesthetics, ethics, and other branches of philosophy as meaningless and redundant. They sought to demarcate physics from metaphysics, in order to consign the latter to uselessness. But Popper was deeply critical of this view, primarily because he felt that many of the most innovative *scientific* discoveries in history began as *metaphysical* statements. 'Scientific research,' he argued, 'is probably impossible without . . . "metaphysical" faith in sometimes hazy theoretical ideas' (Popper, 1935/2007a; 38). Moreover, he argued, 'all observation involves interpretation in the light of our theoretical knowledge . . . pure observational knowledge, unadulterated by theory, would if at all possible, be utterly barren and futile' (Popper, 1963/2007b; 30). Metaphysics was not useless, he believed; rather, it represented the basis for many claims which would go on to become scientific. Scientific knowledge was more advanced than metaphysical knowledge, he believed, and scientists 'may exclude, in a piecemeal fashion, the remaining metaphysical elements in theories, by demarcating them through testability' (Hacohen, 2000; 247). So metaphysics was not meaningless, but rather an important aspect of scientific discovery. Popper therefore believed that, in seeking to consign metaphysics to the rubbish bin, the logical positivists 'failed to notice that they were throwing their *scientific* theories on the same scrapheap as the "meaningless" metaphysical theories' (Popper, 1963/2007b; 349). Consequently, the task was not to demarcate physics from metaphysics, but to demarcate 'science' from 'pseudo-science'; that is, to work out which areas of knowledge fell within the realm of science and which did not.

So for Popper, the problem with the logical positivism of the Vienna Circle was that they were trying to demarcate the wrong things for the wrong reasons. But that was not all. He also believed they were using the wrong criteria of demarcation. The Circle were besotted with Wittgenstein; they read the *Tractatus* line by line (more than once) in their meetings, over the course of a year; they pored over every nuance and detail; Moritz Schlick, along with several other members of the Circle, developed a personal relationship with Wittgenstein and formed an informal discussion group at which they would gain the benefit of the great man's wisdom. Popper loathed him. He considered his whole philosophy to be mistaken and, worse, entirely contrary to what philosophy should be about. Wittgenstein became Popper's nemesis. His central claim that there are no such things as philosophical 'problems' only philosophical 'puzzles' arising from the use of language, and that philosophy was about the pursuit of meaning rather than truth, embodied everything that Popper hated about the self-indulgence of philosophers. For someone who grew up in a city divided by anti-Semitism, poverty, and conflict, who lived through World War I and witnessed the destruction of the Habsburg Empire, the food and fuel shortages, and the revolution first hand, the claim that there were no philosophical 'problems', only 'puzzles', smacked all too obviously of the cosseted world of the coffee house, the fashionable affluent classes, and the irresponsible fripperies of the rich and idle. Popper believed that real philosophical problems existed and that it was the role of the philosopher to seek resolutions to these problems. He believed that philosophy was the search for truth, not meaning. This sense – that

philosophers should concern themselves with the resolution
of concrete problems that exist in the world – informs every
aspect of Popper's philosophy, from the questions he took to be
important, to the way he sought to resolve them. The key was
not to demarcate between what was meaningful and what was
not, but between what provided grounds for knowledge and
what did not.

Popper had begun this project in his PhD thesis, and in his
1929 thesis on geometry. But it was in 1934, with the publication
of *Logik der Forschung* (later translated as *The Logic of Scientific
Discovery*) that Popper famously outlined his alternative theory
of demarcation, and his critique of the foundations upon which
logical positivism were built. What Popper proposed was nothing less than the re-interpretation of science not as an inductive
process, but a deductive one. The problem with the logical positivists, he claimed, was not that they sought to apply the methods
of the physical sciences to philosophy, but that they had a mistaken understanding of what science was, and how it should
be understood. Popper believed that this error was shared by
many scientists, who on the whole clung to Newton's idea that
it was possible to extrapolate generalizable laws of nature from
specific experiments or tests. Popper criticized this view by criticizing the inductive method on which it was based, and turning
it on its head. He did so by applying a Humean scepticism
towards induction itself, and defining science as a deductive
process. Building on his claim that scientific discovery often
begins in metaphysical claims, Popper argued that the inductive
process of discovery (in which scientists move from facts to
general theories) should be inverted: scientific discovery begins
with the statement of theories which are either confirmed or
falsified by facts or other theories. On this view, the truth of any
particular theory (however compelling) is always conjectural
and hypothetical, never irrefutable or concrete. A scientific
theory is a claim about some aspect of the world and, hence,
represents an invitation to others to test and falsify its core
assertions. If it can stand firm against these attempts, then its

claim to truth remains valid (but still hypothetical, as it may be falsified in the future). If it cannot, then it is abandoned. Scientific discovery is thus a process of building and falsifying theories through a process of trial and error. The result was a genuinely new approach to the philosophy of science which had implications for the pursuit of knowledge outside of the scientific community, and which had the potential to empower philosophers and social scientists (as well as scientists) to engage with fundamental problems by employing the same approach. The point was not to determine what was scientific and what was not in order to renounce the latter; rather, it was to provide a broad theory of epistemology, within which it was possible to determine what appropriately belonged to the realm of science and what did not. Consequently, Popper's approach reclaimed non-scientific forms of philosophy as valid pursuits. It also solved many of the problems faced by the Vienna Circle by providing a 'deductive science that was empirical but not inductive, testable and confirmable but not certain, demarcated from metaphysics by falsifiability but not deeming metaphysics meaningless. Science left space for epistemology, methodology, and "non-scientific" philosophy' (Hacohen, 2000; 199).

'A fighting book'

In his *Autobiography*, Popper proclaimed logical positivism dead by his own hand. Logical positivism, he said, collapsed under the weight of 'insuperable internal difficulties. Most of these difficulties had been pointed out in my *Logik der Forschung*. Some members of the Circle were impressed by the need to make changes. Thus the seeds were sown. They led, in the course of many years, to the disintegration of the Circle's tenets' (Popper, 1974/2002; 99). But, as Popper also pointed out, the Circle had begun to dissolve even before its tenets. Interwar Vienna had been becoming increasingly inhospitable to intellectuals, especially those who held left-wing sympathies, or were

Jewish. The economic depression which began in 1929 further divided an already tense society, and ushered in an era of right-wing extremism. A dramatic fall in industrial production, a weakened trades union movement, and a doubling of unemployment between 1929 and 1932 brought economic hardship to many and fresh political challenges to the coalition government. Post-war inflation reached unprecedented levels, wiping out long term savings, and throwing many families into poverty (Popper's father lost his savings in this way). Anti-Semitism, already a visible force in Viennese society – became more vicious and widespread. All Austrian political parties used anti-Jewish imagery in their propaganda, and the Jews bore the brunt of public hostility in the wake of economic chaos. As Hacohen puts it, in the 'Bourgeois imagination, the Jew embodied capitalism, socialism, and the republic, all at the same time' (Hacohen, 2000; 294).

The early 1930s saw the rise of the National Socialists, as the 'white collar German middle class, the civil servants, the German intelligentsia, the non-Jewish professionals, and the petty bourgeoisie' all became supporters of the Nazi cause (Hacohen, 2000; 296–7). The German National Socialists came to power in Berlin on 30 January 1933, and within three months the leader of the Austrian coalition government (which opposed the Nazis) had suspended parliamentary democracy and declared presidential rule. The move was accompanied by a raft of repressive measures, including press censorship, the outlawing of strikes, and the banning of mass public demonstrations. When the socialists failed to stage a fight back, it was clear that a pivotal moment had been reached. In 1934 Englebert Dollfuss (prime minister, and head of the coalition government) created a one party state, and was assassinated by the Nazis on 25th July of that year.

With political and economic tensions reaching boiling point, and threats of German occupation in the air, the philosophers, scientists, and mathematicians of the Vienna Circle joined the doctors, bankers, artists, film-makers, and others in their flight from Austria. Carnap moved to Prague and then joined Godel at Princeton, Menger moved to the University of Notre Dame in Indiana, Hempel went to New York via Brussels and Chicago, Feigle went to Minnesota via Iowa, and Friedrich Waissman moved to Cambridge and then Oxford. Neurath – the most politically active of the Circle – left Vienna for Holland, before settling for the rest of his life in Britain.

Popper left Vienna for New Zealand in 1937, whereupon he took up his first full-time lectureship at Canterbury University College. This was preceded by an extended lecture tour of England during which he met many of the leading lights of British academic life, including A. J. Ayer, Isaiah Berlin, Gilbert Ryle, Bertrand Russell, R. B. Braithwaite, and G. E. Moore, and spoke at many universities on topics arising from *Logik der Forschung*. His most pivotal meeting, although he may not have realized it at the time, was with Friedrich von Hayek, an Austrian émigré economist, and Professor at the London School of Economics. Hayek invited Popper to present to a seminar that he ran at the LSE, and it was at this meeting that Popper chose to develop a number of ideas that he had been toying with about the methodology of the social sciences. The paper, entitled 'The Poverty of Historicism' would later become the book of the same name, and would see Popper apply many of the arguments he had made in *Logik* about science and epistemology to the study of society and politics. Hayek had read *Logik* and was greatly impressed by it. Popper's rejection of social, economic, and political planning proved congenial to Hayek, whose brand of *laissez-faire* free-market economics emerged out of his concerns about epistemological uncertainty. Hayek and Popper worried about similar things: the threat to individual liberty posed by utopian political ideologies; the uncertain nature of human knowledge; the fallibility of reason; the impossibility of knowing another individual's interests more fully or more rationally than the individual him/herself knew them; and, perhaps most of all, the need to ensure that the state did not overstep its bounds, or claim legitimacy in some goal which was valid for all individuals. Hayek and Popper made quite an impression upon one another; an impression which would stay with Hayek sufficiently for him to support Popper in his move to the LSE after the war.

By the time he left for New Zealand, upon returning to Vienna after his sojourn around England, Popper was all but ready to formulate his major contribution to political philosophy. The pieces were nearly all in place. Born into a city of intellectuals and surrounded by progressive socialists, and having lived through the disintegration of all that he had once taken for granted in the destructive energies of war, revolution, and internal conflict, Popper's journey to *The Open Society* had been a slow but inexorable one. Popper was furious at the arrogance of the Austrian Marxists, who failed to notice that interwar economic strife was not leading to socialist revolution, but fascism, and a reactionary politics of hatred and division. He believed that the socialists had deluded themselves: rather than change their tactics in response to the events that were unfolding around them in the 1930s, they remained blinded by their ideology and the false prophecies of Marx that capitalism would end and be replaced by communism. Rather than face the truth, they carried on regardless, interpreting all events and developments as stages on the road to communism. Their hopes were in vain, however, and Popper believed that their failure was not merely a failure of Austrian socialism, but of socialism more broadly. When Popper arrived in New Zealand, his separation from Vienna was merely geographical. His mind was on the political and social world he had left behind. When, in March 1938, the Nazis occupied Austria, Popper heard that many of his family and friends had fallen to the new regime; many were arrested, interrogated and never heard from again, or taken to concentration camps or prison. His mother died in May 1938, and his sister escaped to Paris in June, without money or passport. 'Other relatives and friends were scrambling to leave the country, to England, France, anywhere – even New Zealand' (Hacohen, 2000; 345). According to Hacohen, Popper, with his friend Otto Frankael, did what he could to organize immigration permits for Austrians to come to New Zealand, but there were many obstacles to doing so.

In the face of such overwhelming horror and uncertainty, Popper's mind turned from natural science to politics. Unlike Wittgenstein, who believed that philosophy could have nothing to say about political or social problems, Popper felt that philosophy as *he* understood it could contribute to the fight against tyranny, and against the rising tide of fascism. With the outbreak of World War II, Popper put aside what was to become *The Poverty of Historicism* and began work on another book which would draw on many of its central themes. Together these books would represent Popper's 'war effort'. *The Open Society*, especially, he described as a 'fighting book'.

Given the contemporary neglect of *The Open Society* by political philosophers, it is easy to underestimate how radical and important the book was at the time of its publication. Popper's aim was nothing less than to trace the origins of the totalitarian ideologies which dominated world politics at that time, and had produced the greatest evils that the world had ever known. His conclusion was that these origins could be traced back to some of the most celebrated and revered figures in the history of Western civilization. Prior to *The Open Society*, Ancient Greece had been largely held by classicists and historians as the seat of enlightened democracy and culture, and Plato, its most notable and eloquent voice, as an embodiment of reason and humanity. Hegel – whose philosophy was considered controversial and difficult – was nevertheless considered a philosopher of major significance. And Marx – controversial, problematic, and politically explosive – was seen by many as a first-rate economist, and revered by academics and others for providing a systematic diagnosis of inequality and political injustice worthy not only of study but, for many, of dedicating one's life to. Popper found them all guilty of paving the way for the tyranny and evil found at the heart of fascism and Nazism: Plato was painted as a racist, and a self-aggrandizing betrayer of Socrates who hated freedom,

Hegel a clown and a fool who dressed his ridiculous and hateful ideas in an impenetrable cloak of baffling complexity and who pandered to the political leaders of his time in return for money, and Marx a false prophet whose teachings encouraged a generation to believe they were unfree, and powerless before the unstoppable forces of history. The message of the book was clear: that in the work of these great figures, and others who shared their method, we find the justification for tyranny, for murder, for racial politics, for tribalism, for evil – we find the closed society. And in his response, we can glimpse ideas traceable right back to his childhood in Vienna – we can see the influence of the progressives in Popper's rejection of nationalism as being exclusionary and 'closed', his belief in the capacity of individual human beings to change the society in which they live, that the state should aim to alleviate poverty through the implementation of humane social policies, and that it was possible to view science and social technology as a means of understanding social problems and responding to them. We can see his commitment to the ability of individuals to reason productively about their lives, and about the world in which they live, and that it was important for the state (and for teachers) to recognize and encourage this ability. And most obviously, we can see his ideas, expressed in *Logik* and countless other essays and lectures, about knowledge, the process by which individual human beings come to know about the world in which they live, and about the limits to that process which place necessary and inevitable checks on what states can do, and the justifications they can provide for their actions.

The Open Society brought Popper immediate attention, both good and bad. Many derided his scholarship and accused him of caricaturing and misrepresenting the views of Marx, Plato, and Hegel. Despite his support for state intervention in economic markets in the interests of alleviating poverty, the provision of public services and education for all (regardless of income), his rejection of social, economic, or political privilege, his avowal of a deliberative form of democracy open to all, and his commitment to social change through debate and critical engagement on fundamental political assumptions, Marxists condemned him as an establishment figure and an apologist for capitalism. State socialists like Harold Laski supported Popper's conclusions, however, as did many other socialist academics and activists, including Bertrand Russell – an intellectual inspiration to both Popper and to the Vienna Circle – who proclaimed his attack on Plato's philosophy as 'brilliant'. Popper's aim was to 'destroy the unreal and metaphysical gulf that separates reasonable and liberal people in the various camps on the left', and to bind these disparate groups together in a common cause against totalitarianism (Popper, Letter to Alfred Braunthal, 12 December 1943; quoted in Hacohen, 449). But his book became popular with the Right, too. One of its biggest champions was Popper's friend Hayek, who was so impressed that he set out to get Popper a job at the LSE on the strength of it. Popper's defence of piecemeal social engineering in place of utopian planning, and his critique of historicism in politics and the social sciences, fit well with Hayek's general scepticism about epistemological certainty, and his views as to the spontaneity of social and political institutions. Popper's argument was more hospitable to economic interventionism and social planning than Hayek's, but nevertheless, Hayek was impressed by the application of Popper's scientific theory to social and economic questions and believed that he would be the perfect candidate for a position in logic and scientific method at the School. Hayek's efforts paid off, and Popper arrived in Britain on 5 January 1946, following the end of hostilities in Europe, to take up his post at the LSE. In 1949, he was appointed Professor of Logic and Scientific Method, a post he held for 23 years.

The later years

His first few years at the LSE 'were exhilarating. He was a rising star. *The Open Society* threw him overnight into the public eye.

At the LSE he drew large audiences, competing with Laski for popularity' (Hacohen, 2000; 523). Invitations to speak were plentiful. One meeting in particular has become the stuff of legend. On 25 October 1946, Popper presented a paper to a meeting of Cambridge's Moral Sciences Club, attended by a number of leading philosophers, including Bertrand Russell and one Ludwig Wittgenstein. Popper had been asked to present a short paper on 'some philosophical puzzle'. Popper chose to present a paper not-so-innocently entitled 'Are there any philosophical problems?', and used the session to provide a trenchant and sustained critique of Wittgenstein's idea that philosophy was a search for meaning in linguistic puzzles, rather than a search for the resolution of concrete problems. Differing views exist as to what actually transpired during the meeting (Popper's own recollections on the matter have been shown to be unreliable), but what can be gleaned from the testimony of those present is that Wittgenstein challenged Popper to provide examples of philosophical problems rather than puzzles. Popper suggested induction, infinity, and the validity of moral rules. Wittgenstein dismissed these examples and, in his frustration, began toying with a poker that he had taken from the fire in the room (as, apparently, was his habit). When challenged to provide an example of a moral rule, Popper said 'Not to threaten visiting lecturers with pokers', at which point (according to Popper as well as a number of others present), Wittgenstein threw down the poker and left the room. The accuracy of all this is difficult to ascertain, but it is certainly clear that Popper relished the opportunity, finally, to face his nemesis and show his philosophy to be mistaken. It was not a view that Wittgenstein was used to hearing.

The Open Society cut across ideological divides and united many liberals and socialists against nationalism, tribalism, and tyranny, and in support of individual freedom, equality, and reason. The book became a classic text in what became known – somewhat pejoratively – as 'cold war liberalism', and a canonical rejection of communism. Popper joined with other post-war liberals in trying to convince the trades unions and the socialists that capitalism had been replaced by totalitarianism as the enemy of the people. The cold war hostility towards communism mandated a consensus among liberals, socialists, and libertarians against the common enemy, and Popper's defence of piecemeal social engineering and democracy provided a rallying point.

As time went on, however, Popper's attitude towards democracy began to change. Mass support for fascist and illiberal parties around the world led him (and other post-war liberals) to worry about the compatibility of freedom and democracy. Post-war liberals became increasingly sceptical of the claim that democracy was the best way of securing individual freedom. Popper remained an advocate of democracy, but chose to redefine it as a thin rather than substantive idea. He did not think that it was based on the idea that the majority should rule, or that decision-making power should be devolved down to the citizen body, or that the citizen body need necessarily participate in political activity; indeed, Popper held that public opinion was an 'irresponsible form of power' and a 'danger to freedom if it is not moderated by a strong liberal tradition' (Popper, 1963/2007b; 476). Rather, it was merely a system of checks and balances which allowed for the peaceful removal of tyrants. Popper therefore seemed to subordinate democracy to liberalism. In doing so, critics have suggested that Popper was moving to the political right (Hacohen).

This view was strengthened, perhaps, in the light of Popper's later pronouncements concerning liberal tolerance, which he believed mandated the silencing of illiberal, intolerant groups: '[A]ny movement preaching intolerance places itself outside the law', he argued, and hence, could reasonably be suppressed (Popper, 1945/2006a; 292–4). Such suppression was seen as a last resort, however, and post-war liberals generally favoured open dialogue as the means by which differences might be resolved and diverse interests represented. Critics claimed that such a view was idealistic and, again, represented a move towards conservatism, as dominant majorities would always marginalize the needs of minority groups. The picture of democracy that Popper presented in *The Open Society* and in later essays was seen by some as too abstract, and insufficiently attentive to the power held by majorities, and the lack of power held by minorities, to shape the political agenda and to voice their concerns. And there was a more fundamental problem: how could Popper's theory of knowledge and discovery, which was premised upon constant refutation, debate, and critique, possibly yield the kind of agreements and compromises necessary in politics? Conservative thinkers like Carl Schmitt have suggested that in the face of unresolvable disagreement and never-ending democratic dialogue, real decisions are in fact made by powerful elites behind closed doors. Popper's defence of an idealized deliberative democracy failed to provide a compelling defence against such a charge, and hence, his defence of democracy has been considered by some to be a de facto defence of elite rule.

In 1950, Popper moved to a house in rural Penn, Buckinghamshire, on the outskirts of London. Despite continuing to work on political matters, especially the relationship between liberalism and socialism, Popper's mind returned to the philosophy of science. With increased seclusion, those political ideas that Popper developed did indeed seem more conservative, although the application of ideological labels to Popper's political vision is difficult, as we will see. His 1954 essay 'Public opinion and liberal principles', quoted earlier, was indicative of this, as were his essays 'Toleration and Intellectual Responsibility' and 'What Does the West Believe in?', in which he extolled the virtues of liberal democracy as the best form of government ever invented. He was effusive in his praise of Hayek's *The Constitution of Liberty*, published in 1960, which forced Popper to confront the tensions in his own work between his defence of social engineering and his support for a limited state. His response was to become much more sceptical about state intervention and to cling more strongly to the emancipatory power of democracy and liberty as a grounds for piecemeal social reform.

The years following the publication of *The Open Society* were a time of professional triumphs and personal change. He was elected as a Fellow of the British Academy in 1958 and knighted in 1965. In the same year, the City of Vienna awarded him the *Geisteswissenschaften Prize*, and would later celebrate his 80th birthday with symposia and awards. He was elected as a Fellow of the Royal Society in 1976. However, Popper became even more isolated from his fellow philosophers, many of whom he believed were engaged in irrelevancies. Although his appearances at the LSE became less regular, his influence remained strong. Following the publication of Thomas Kuhn's groundbreaking *The Structure of Scientific Revolutions* in 1962, Popper responded with 'The myth of the framework', in which he provided a trenchant critique of Kuhn's 'incommensurability of theses' argument, a strident critique of cultural and political relativism, and a defence of political deliberation and reason which resonates with the work of later liberal thinkers like John Rawls, Jeremy Waldron, and Joshua Cohen.

Popper became increasingly separated not merely from the LSE but from the world at large. His furious critique of critical theory, and his angry denunciation of such theorists as Jurgen Habermas, Theodor Adorno, and Max Horkheimer, seemed to cement his move to the Right, and distanced him from a lot of what came to be associated with Leftist politics during the 1960s and 1970s. Similarly, his claim that people needed to work with existing political institutions and practices in order to reform them from the inside rather than challenge them directly seemed at odds with the growing tendency among supporters of the Left to adopt more direct, radical approaches to social change, like forming protest movements or participating in demonstrations. The political and social climate in the 1970s brought out his conservative sympathies even more starkly: he often raged against the 'New Left, the British public health system, . . . and the British labour unions' suicidal tactics' (Hacohen, 2000; 540). However, it was clear that Popper's knowledge of world affairs was sketchy. 'When, in his final years, he watched a little television, he was horrified by both the programs and the media's power, and suggested controlling them in ways which violated liberal principles.' (Hacohen, 2000; 540). The failures of British socialism in the 1970s appeared the last straw for Popper, who had been increasingly convinced by Hayek and others of the potential tensions between the principles of individual freedom and equality. By 1974 – and perhaps earlier – Popper's transition from progressive socialist, to communist, to social democrat, and finally to conservative liberal, was, for many, obvious and complete. Looking back on this journey in this *Autobiography*, Popper eloquently states why he gave up on socialism and its promise of equality. 'I remained a socialist for many years, even after my rejection of Marxism,' he wrote,

> and if there could be such a thing as socialism combined with liberty then I would be a socialist still. For nothing could be better than living a modest, simple and free life in an egalitarian society. It took some time before I recognized this as no more than a beautiful dream; that freedom is more important than equality, that the attempt to realize equality endangers freedom; and that, if freedom is lost, there will not even be equality among the unfree. (Popper, 1974/2002; 36)

Read at face value, this paragraph seems to support the popular notion that Popper ended his political journey as a libertarian, or as what had become known as the conservatism of Margaret Thatcher, Ronald Reagan, and the New Right. But the story is not so simple. True, Popper's rejection of socialist equality in this passage is emphatic, but his political philosophy (both early and late) is characterized by a search for a humane society in which freedom and equality might coexist *together*. True, he defends individual freedom, a limited state, and reasonable discussion as a means of resolving cultural and ethnic differences; and true, he argues that there may be grounds for not tolerating illiberal groups, denying that certain unreasonable claims or ideas need to be excluded from public debate, and that liberalism and democracy may not be entirely compatible. But these are ideas that are now shared by many contemporary egalitarian liberals, who are neither conservatives nor libertarians. He may have remained a committed individualist at a time when political discourse was becoming dominated by talk of groups, movements, and social activism, but the claim that individuals (and not groups) should be considered the principal actors in a democratic state does not necessarily imply conservatism. Indeed, such a position is entirely compatible with non-socialist understandings of equality, and has been advanced by many liberals who claim to be interested in supporting both freedom *and* equality. Popper's rejection of equality in the above passage is thus curious: despite his worries about the capacity of socialism to establish equality, he did not seem to give up on the idea of equality per se. At no point in his early or late political philosophy does he defend a society in which individual freedom is considered the only virtue to be encouraged; he defends a vision of society as 'open' rather than 'closed', a vision in which the capacity of *all* individual human beings to live free and flourishing lives is celebrated and nurtured, and in which arbitrary distinctions between the 'deserving' and the 'undeserving', the 'worthy' and the 'unworthy', are rejected and replaced with an appeal to cosmopolitanism and universalism. At the heart of Popper's critique of irrationalism in *The Open Society*, after all, was that it assumed 'the inequality of men'. It cannot be denied that 'human beings are, like all other things in our world, in very many respects very unequal,' he argued. 'Nor can it be doubted that this inequality is of great importance and even in many respects highly desirable. But all this has no bearing on the question whether or not we should treat men, especially in political issues, as equals, or as much like equals as possible: that is to say, as possessing equal rights, and equal claims to equal treatment; and it has no bearing upon the question of whether we ought to construct political institutions accordingly. "Equality before the law" is not a fact but a political demand based upon a moral decision' (Popper 1945/2006b; 259). The paradox that runs throughout Popper's political thought, then, and an important issue that crops up time and again in his discussion of it, is this central relationship between equality and freedom, and the extent to which his original progressive vision of an egalitarian society free from poverty might be reconciled with a society premised upon individual freedom (from the state, from others, and from one's own ignorance).

By the time Popper died on 17 September 1994, many believed that he had abandoned this project, but in fact, his commitment to the values which underpin his old egalitarianism were still evident. True, he moved away from social technology as an appropriate response to resolving political problems, and voiced concerns about mass democracy; he united with cold war liberals who sought to champion liberal principles on the world stage, and his politics became increasingly defined in reaction to Soviet excesses and the spread of illiberal groups who threatened freedom. But despite all this, his commitment to individual freedom, the possibility of advancing knowledge through human endeavour, and his distrust of assumed knowledge and authority were unwavering. In Popper's later politics, as in his earlier work, we find a hatred of tribal and nationalist conservatism, a rejection of privilege, and a genuine belief in the capacity of all people – if given the chance and the right resources – to free themselves from the grip of ignorance, tyranny, and the inequalities of wealth and power which thwart their lives. It is this belief – in the enlightenment, in reason, and in the equal dignity of all human beings – which is so relevant to contemporary politics and philosophy, and which resonates with so much contemporary political theory in the twenty-first century.

2

Popper's Ideas

Popper wrote widely and prolifically over the course of his long career, on a range of diverse subjects. His principal interest, however, and the mission which drove and unified his work in areas as divergent as music, history, logic, mathematics, science, social science, and politics, was the 'problem of cosmology: the problem of understanding the world – including ourselves, and our knowledge, as part of the world' (Popper 1935/2007a; xix).

Popper believed that this was the central problem of philosophy. In arguing as much, he saw himself as belonging to a long and noble tradition of rationalist philosophers for whom the pursuit of knowledge (about the world and, importantly, about knowledge itself) was of crucial importance. From 'Plato to Descartes, Leibniz, Kant, Duhem and Poincaré; and from Bacon, Hobbes, and Locke, to Hume, Mill, and Russell, the theory of knowledge was inspired by the hope that it would enable us not only to know more about knowledge, but also to contribute to the advance of knowledge', and *scientific* knowledge in particular. It was a hope that Popper shared. And in sharing it, he set himself against the logical positivists of the Vienna Circle and 'ordinary language' philosophers like J. L. Austin and Gilbert Ryle who both, in their own ways, held that philosophy was primarily the study of language. 'Most of the philosophers who believe that the characteristic method of philosophy is the analysis of ordinary language seem to have lost the admirable optimism which once inspired the rationalist tradition', he wrote. 'Their attitude, it seems, has become one of resignation, if not despair' (Popper, 1935/2007a; xxii).

Popper's philosophy should be read as an attempt to counsel against this despair, and to overturn what he saw as the flawed philosophical doctrines which cause it. We have already mentioned some of them in Chapter 1 (the rejection of psychologism, logical positivism, Wittgensteinean linguistic philosophy, and the idea that philosophy is appropriately understood as the search for meaning rather than the resolution of concrete problems in the world), and we will discuss several more in the chapters which follow. Popper's aim was to establish an *epistemology* – a theory which would explain the status and growth of knowledge in the world, and which could be applied to all areas of human endeavour in which knowledge is sought. It was not, as it was for the logical positivists, to demarcate 'physics' from 'metaphysics' in order to junk the latter, but to demarcate science from pseudo-science (that is, to demarcate scientific theories from those theories which purported to be scientific but in fact were not). His conclusions were radical and far-reaching, and informed not only his work on science, logic, and mathematics, but politics and social science too. It is not possible to provide an exhaustive treatment of Popper's philosophy of science here, as this book is principally concerned with his political philosophy. I will therefore flesh out some of the ideas described in the previous chapter, in particular those aspects of his epistemology which bear most importantly upon his political philosophy, before discussing the ways in which he applied these ideas first to the study of society (in *The Poverty of Historicism*) and then to politics (in *The Open Society and Its Enemies*). Having done so, I will, in Chapter 3, discuss some of the ways in which his political views changed in the years following the publication of *The Open Society*.

Popper's epistemology

Popper believed that 'the central problem of epistemology has always been . . . the problem of the growth of knowledge.

And the growth of knowledge', he argued, 'can be studied best by studying the growth of scientific knowledge' (Popper, 1935/ 2007a; xix). So how, and by what method, does scientific knowledge grow? How are scientific discoveries made?

According to the traditional view, science is an *inductive* process in which scientists begin by collating and systematizing observations about the world in order to extrapolate from their observations overarching laws of nature. These laws of nature can in turn be used to *explain* the world (by verifying certain claims about it), and to *predict* future events. Consequently, science begins in the *observation* of certain natural properties or behaviours (in elements or chemicals like, say, lead, or water, or hydrogen, or in physical objects like wheels or propellers or atoms). In particular, it begins in the observation of particular, isolatable properties or behaviours via scientific experiments. The results (observations) gathered during these experiments are used to infer generalizable laws. It is therefore an important job of the scientist to establish the appropriate circumstances in which the observations might be made and tested in ways which do not lead to unintended or tainted consequences. Scientific *theories* are thus *inferred* from observed *facts* about the world, which are gathered through a process of repeated experimentation and empirical testing under controlled conditions. The resultant theories have a *predictive* and *verificational* quality: by isolating and observing the specific behaviour of specific objects (for example, the effect of gravity upon a falling apple), it is possible to *verify* (or *prove*) the truth of a claim about the world (e.g. the statement 'apples do not fall upwards'), and *predict* future events (e.g. 'if I were to release my grip on this apple, it would fall downwards'). Theories can be *proven*, or *justified*, by appropriately observed facts, and scientific progress is driven by, and measured in terms of, the growth in the number of such theories. The more the theory can explain in this way – the more universal its applicability – the more important it is considered.

This view of the scientific method – as an inductive process of establishing general laws of nature from specific, observable

facts – has a long and illustrious pedigree, is generally held by
the majority of scientists, and is held to be exemplified in the
work of many of the greatest scientists in history, including
Galileo, Copernicus, Kepler, and Isaac Newton. Newton's observation of something as small and insignificant as a falling apple,
for example, allowed him to develop a general theory of universal gravitation which further allowed him to explain the movement of the planets, and predict their future progress, with
great success and precision. The groundbreaking significance
of Newton's theory for many lay primarily in the fact that it
was rooted in *observations* of particular events or properties, but
could be applied to all physical objects. From specific observations of specific objects, Newton was able to derive laws of nature
which were generalizable and universal, and which could therefore contribute to a broad and far-reaching system of rules
concerning the basic structure of the universe. Scientists before
and after have employed an inductive method in their search
for truth about the world and the wider cosmos in the hope that
their observations will allow them to derive similarly universal
and generalizable laws, capable of both explaining and predicting events.

Popper believed that this traditional understanding of science
was fundamentally flawed. His reasons were various. *First*, he
argued that the inductive method relies on a fundamental philosophical and logical impossibility, namely, that the 'truth of . . .
[a] theory could be logically derived from the truth of certain
observation-statements' (Popper, 1963/2007b; 251). Popper
argued, on the contrary, that '[n]o rule can ever guarantee that
a generalization inferred from true observations, however often
repeated, is true' (Popper, 1963/2007b; 71). He did so by appealing to Hume's critique of induction in his *Enquiry into Human
Understanding*. In that book, Hume states that there are no valid
arguments allowing us to establish 'that those instances, of which
we have had no experience, resemble those, of which we have
had experience'. Consequently, Hume states, 'even after the
observation of the frequent or constant conjunction of objects,

we have no reason to draw any inference concerning any object beyond those of which we have had experience'; thus we should not 'form any conclusion beyond those past instances, of which we have had experience' (quoted in Popper 1963/2007b; 55–6). In other words, the fact that something has happened in the past, even a hundred or a thousand or a million times, does not mean it will happen in the same way in the future: repeated observations of a particular event under particular circumstances cannot *prove* inconclusively that it will always occur in the way we expect, or at all. We cannot predict the future by examining the past, however sure we are that we have observed the past correctly, and identified regularities or trends in it.

This claim led Popper to a radical conclusion: that the long-standing view that scientists should seek to derive generalizable laws of nature from specific events or facts in the world is mistaken and futile. Moreover, he concluded, the problem of induction implies that any theories we develop can never be scientifically *proven* – they can only be *falsified*. The statement 'All swans are white' cannot be *proven* by observing any number of white swans, but it can be decisively *falsified* by observing one non-white swan. The claim 'The fortress is impregnable' cannot be *proven* by any number of unsuccessful attempts to breach its defences, but it can be decisively *refuted* by a single successful attempt. And the theory that the sun will not rise in the morning unless a sacrifice is made to the sun god (as the Aztecs believed) cannot be *proven* by any number of successful sacrifices, but can be decisively *refuted* by the fact of the sun rising when no sacrifice was made. Facts cannot *prove* a theory to be true, but they can show it to be *false*. And once shown to be false, a theory comes to represent a genuine contribution to knowledge: we can state what is *not* true much more definitively than we can state what *is* true, and consequently, refuted statements are valuable. They are not useless (as the traditional view holds); for Popper the refutation of a theory represents a real advance in scientific knowledge which should be celebrated and valued because finding out that a theory *cannot* be true is an important step in what *is*, or *can be*, true. Useless theories, on the other hand, are those theories which cannot be falsified. Given that it is not possible to provide irrefutable proofs, or certain truths, in the realm of science (given the problem of induction), theories framed *as if* they were irrefutable truths, and which admit no possibility of falsification, are thus unscientific and unhelpful. Consider, for example, two statements:

(a) Because we have provided this sacrifice, it will rain tomorrow.
(b) Because we have provided this sacrifice, it will rain in the future.

What makes (a) a possible candidate for the truth (and hence, *scientific*) and (b) *unscientific* is that (a) can be refuted while (b) cannot. That is, we may not *currently* possess the requisite knowledge to refute it, but it is framed in such a way that we *may* one day do so. Statement (a) is precise while (b) is imprecise. Statement (a)'s precision means that it can be tested (by waiting until tomorrow to see if it rains), while (b)'s imprecision means that it cannot: we can spend generations waiting for it to rain but, given that it is possible to do so infinitely, we will never know if it will or not. Consequently, (b) is incapable of adding anything to our knowledge of the world, while (a) is capable of doing so (although it still may not be true). Popper believed that predictions (in science as elsewhere) are important and possible, but that they must be precise and, hence, falsifiable, rather than general and unfalsifiable. They also need to be short-term. Reason can be predictive, but it is necessarily limited and fallible. No individual or group of individuals can foresee all the various long-term consequences of particular actions or reactions by reasoning about them; consequently, predictions must be tentative and short-term, rather than radical and long-term. Science cannot and should not seek to establish theories which prove certain things about the world (that is, which *verify* the truth of a statement or claim) – rather, it should seek to eliminate error in those falsifiable theories which currently exist. Moreover, the fact that theories cannot be *proven* to be true, means that all existing theories – however compelling or persuasive or universally applicable – must be considered inherently conjectural and hypothetical: as no hypothesis can be proven, it remains forever a *hypothesis* (unless it is ever shown to be false, in which case it is abandoned).

Secondly, and relatedly, Popper disputed the philosophical and historical accuracy of the view that science begins in *observation*. Popper believed, on the contrary, that science begins with the proposal of *theories* concerning particular *problems*. This represented an inversion of the traditional inductive understanding of science: while inductivists held that science moves from observations (or facts) to theories (or general laws), Popper argued that science in fact begins with the identification of *problems* about which we propose *theories* which may in turn be *falsified* by other theories or observations. This connects with the point raised in Chapter 1: that, for Popper, the growth of knowledge arises out of our confrontation with real problems rather than, say, the meaning of linguistic statements. Science, he held, was not an *inductive* process, but a *deductive* one: scientists identify certain problems in the world, propose theories to resolve them, and then seek to falsify these theories. If they can falsify them, then they are abandoned (except for any residual elements which stand up to testing); if they cannot, then the theory stands while they continue to seek refutations based upon what is currently known: such theories cannot be considered true, but they may be considered hypothetically true, or potentially true. That is, facts are not used to prove theories, and they are not considered a source for general laws of nature, rather, they are used to deduce whether or not a particular theory can be correct given what is currently known about the world. Science, then, does not begin in observation, but in the positing of *theories* about *problems*.

Again, the implications of this for our understanding of science are radical and far-reaching. It has become an assumed truth that science is (and should be) characterized by a dispassionate, clinical detachment from the world, and understood as a process of observation, experimentation, and collation of results in a controlled environment. This, Popper believed, was characteristic of a particular brand of the rationalist tradition exemplified by Bacon and Descartes, who argued that in order to understand the world we must first 'purge our minds of all conjectures or guesses or prejudices' which might taint our findings, and reveal truth by the light of our reason alone (Popper, 1963/2007b; 19). It was also, as we saw in Chapter 1, the view of the logical positivists. Popper, on the other hand, believed that scientific discoveries do not arise from the barren application of reason in the world, but precisely in those conjectures and guesses and prejudices which Bacon, Descartes, and the logical positivists urged us to put aside. 'Science must begin . . . neither with the collection of observations, nor with the invention of experiments,' Popper argued, 'but with the critical discussion of myths' (Popper, 1963/2007b; 66). Human beings are inclined to impose order upon the world and their lives by trying to explain them, and in particular, by trying to explain them in terms of regularities or trends on which they can depend, and which can be used to explain current events, and predict events in the future. This is true of children (as Popper argued in his 1927 thesis, written at the Pedagogic Institute), and of adults too; it is evident in our desire to establish overarching natural laws, but also in our construction of other myths and narratives which provide order and context to our lives: for example, myths of nation, religion, culture, history. These myths and conventions are important in that they set the initial framework within which scientific investigations are conducted. 'Observation is always selective', Popper argued. 'It needs a chosen object, a definite task, an interest, a point of view, a problem' (Popper 1963/2007b; 61). It is not the job of the scientist to collect random observations about the world, but to solve problems by attempting to falsify those conjectural solutions (or theories) which already exist. In science as elsewhere, we 'cannot know: we can only guess. And our guesses are guided by the unscientific, the metaphysical (though biologically explainable) faith in laws, in regularities which we can uncover' (Popper 1935/2007a; 275). Scientists cannot merely *look* (or listen, or hear, or feel), they need to know what they are looking *for*, and how they might look *effectively*. Similarly, they cannot merely *create*: they need some context of ends (some problem requiring a solution) which can guide them. 'No amount of physics will tell a scientist that it is the right thing for him to construct a plough, or an aeroplane, or an atomic bomb', Popper wrote. 'Ends must be adopted by him, or given to him; and what he does *qua* scientist is only to construct means by which these ends can be realized' (Popper 1963/2007b; 483). Theory thus 'dominates the experimental work from its initial planning up to the finishing touches in the laboratory' (Popper 1935/2007a; 90).

Furthermore, for Popper, the idea that scientific discovery begins in *observation* rather than the proposal of *theories* (often rooted in myths and metaphysical ideas) is simply not true of some of the most significant advances in the history of cosmology. 'For it is a fact', Popper wrote, 'that purely metaphysical ideas . . . have been of the greatest importance for cosmology. From Thales to Einstein, from ancient atomism to Descartes's speculations about matter, from the speculations of Gilbert and Newton and Leibniz and Boscovic about forces to those of Faraday and Einstein about fields of forces, metaphysical ideas have shown the way' (Popper, 1935/2007a; xxiii). 'Copernicus's idea of placing the sun rather than the earth in the centre of the universe', for example, 'was not the result of new observations but of a *new interpretation* of old and well-known facts in the light of semi-religious Platonic and neo-Platonic ideas' concerning the pre-eminence of the sun in the natural order. Thus, he says, the Copernican revolution in astronomy did not 'start with observations, but with a religious or mythological idea' (Popper, 1963/2007b; 253–4). Similarly, Kepler's claim that the planets held an elliptical orbit around the sun and that their velocities changed throughout their journey did not arise from observations, but from a desire to prove the *pre-existing* theory that the planets held a circular orbit and travelled at a constant velocity. And Einstein's quantum theory was incredibly speculative and abstract, and could not – Popper believed – be appropriately said to be based upon specific observations at all. Therefore, if the claim – shared by many scientists, in addition to the logical positivists of the Vienna Circle – that science is rooted principally in an accumulation of sense-experiences (or observations) and, hence, is inimical to metaphysical theorizing were correct then none of these theories, as well as countless others, could be understood as truly 'scientific'. The irony of the position advanced by the logical positivists, then, was that they held science to be pre-eminent over philosophy (and sought to demarcate valid and invalid philosophical enquiry by appealing to the inductive scientific method) only to define science (and, therefore, their understanding of philosophy) 'in such a way that it [became], by definition, incapable of making any contribution to our knowledge of the world', and unable, too, to include many of history's most important scientific discoveries (Popper, 1935/2007a; xii).

Science is therefore no enemy of metaphysical theorizing, because metaphysics and settled conviction often provide the springboard for scientific discovery by providing guidance as to what questions the scientist should ask, and how she should ask them. But science *does* represent the means by which we might know *which* metaphysical positions – or which *aspects* of a particular position – are worthy of support. 'Once put forward,' he argued, none of our metaphysical conjectures 'are dogmatically upheld. Our method of research is not to defend them, in order to show how right we were. On the contrary, we try to overthrow them. Using all the weaponry of our logical, mathematical, and technical armoury, we try to prove that our anticipations were false – in order to put forward, in their stead, new unjustified and unjustifiable anticipations, new "rash and premature prejudices" as Bacon derisively called them' (Popper, 1935/2007a;

278–9). Many metaphysical theories will contain erroneous or mistaken claims, but these can be revealed and refuted through critical engagement and perhaps empirical testing. Science (on Popper's understanding) provides the critical tools capable of making metaphysical positions more helpful (by removing those aspects of them which can be shown to be mistaken), but it should not be considered the enemy of these positions, or of metaphysics in general.

Popper thus believed that in solving the problem of induction by reconceptualizing the growth of knowledge as a non-inductive process of testing and discussing theories critically, he had provided a more persuasive answer to the original problem of demarcation posed by the logical positivists of the Vienna Circle. Remember, their claim (with which Popper had a great deal of sympathy) was that philosophy would benefit from the rigour characteristic of the physical sciences, and that the methods of the physical sciences should therefore be applied to philosophy. For the logical positivists, this meant working out which aspects of the *discipline of philosophy* were compatible with – or could be brought within – the methods characteristic of the *discipline of science* (understood in the traditional, inductive way). The scientific method therefore provided a solid basis for demarcating between physics and metaphysics, or science and non-science, and hence, valid and invalid philosophical questions. Popper rejected all of this, turned the inductivist method on its head, and argued that the growth of scientific knowledge proceeded in the same way as knowledge in any other field, and in fact, *relied* on other fields of inquiry. Scientific discovery, like the growth of knowledge in other areas, is unpredictable, often complicated, messy, and problematic; it does not always follow a set pattern and, even if it does, it is not clear that we could predict this pattern beforehand; and it emerges from a process of trial and error, and of rational, critical discussion among a community of peers. The growth of knowledge – in science as elsewhere – is thus a *public* process. Knowledge does not grow merely as a result of those private and isolated endeavours of individual scientists, for example; it grows out of the public discussion and critique of the theories proposed by these individuals. All knowledge (including, but not limited to, *scientific* knowledge) thus grows out of the ongoing critical engagement with problems among individual human beings across many disciplines.

This is what Popper meant when he stated that there was no method peculiar to science: knowledge, in all areas of human endeavour, grows out of the process of individuals engaging with one another over the possible resolution of problems, and the falsification of those theories that already exist. Consequently, Popper was deeply distrustful of the inclination – common in modern academic life, and implicit in the view of the logical positivists – of dividing the search for knowledge into particular disciplinary realms, each governed by their own methodologies and conventions and accepted practices. The urge to create disciplinary sub-divisions of this kind, he believed, arbitrarily fragmented a process of epistemological discovery which should be considered broadly uniform across all disciplines. 'The belief that there is such a thing as physics, or biology, or archaeology, and that these "studies" or "disciplines" are distinguishable by their subject matter which they investigate, appears to me to be a residue from the time when one believed that a theory had to proceed from a definition of its own subject matter', he wrote. 'But subject matter . . . [does] not . . . constitute a basis for distinguishing disciplines.' The portioning up of the general quest for knowledge into discreet disciplinary fields is really little more than a matter of administrative convenience. All such 'classification and distinction is a comparatively unimportant and superficial affair. *We are not students of some subject matter but students of problems.* And problems may cut right across the borders of any subject matter or discipline' (Popper 1963/ 2007b; 88). While some differentiation among disciplines is sometimes helpful, then, members of these disciplines should understand that they are all involved in the same process of discovery, using broadly the same methodology. Questions such as 'What is philosophy?' or 'What is economics?' are redundant, self-indulgent, and merely an off-shoot of the Wittgensteinean desire to search for the meaning of words, or the Aristotelian need to understand phenomena in terms of their 'essences'. Philosophers, scientists, and economists should not seek to determine the 'essence' of their discipline, by distinguishing its methodology from that of others, rather, they should confront problems by adopting a critical attitude towards all existing ideas and theories, and by proposing and falsifying theories through a process of rational, critical discussion – a discussion which is not limited to one set of disciplinary concerns, but which ranges across all disciplines and subject areas. *Scientific* discoveries, for example, may spring – and have sprung – from *religious* theories, or mathematics; and *political* innovations might spring (and have sprung) from theories generally thought to be the preserve of economists, or psychologists, or sociologists. What is important is that those engaged in all these fields do not seek to ring-fence their own endeavours, but instead engage enthusiastically in a critical engagement with these theories (and their proposers) with an open mind. Popper called this 'critical rationalism': the tradition, drawn from the Greeks, 'of [the] free discussion of theories with the aim of discovering their weak spots so that they may be improved'; the idea that individuals from all disciplines should engage with one another over the resolution of problems in the world and that, in these discussions, they should adopt 'an attitude of readiness to listen to critical arguments and to learn from experience' (Popper, 1963/2007b; 67). Critical rationalism is thus fundamentally 'an attitude of admitting that "*I may be wrong and you may be right, and by an effort, we may get nearer to the truth*"' (Popper, 1945/2006b; 249).

In arguing as much, Popper believed that he had provided not just a more coherent definition of the physical sciences, but a broad epistemological theory which could explain the growth of knowledge not just in science, but in all fields and all disciplines. Popper's deductive method suggested that scientists and philosophers who were committed to contributing to our understanding of the world should see themselves as engaged in a common project, rather than different projects which are defined by different methodologies and subject-matters. Scientists and philosophers are (or should be) in the business of confronting and proposing solutions to problems, and engaging with others in critical dialogue about the efficacy or coherence of existing theories as well as the theories that they themselves have proposed. Doing so ensured scientific objectivity. 'The naïve view that scientific objectivity rests on the mental or psychological attitude of the individual scientist, on his training, care, and scientific detachment, generates as a reaction the sceptical view that scientists can never be objective.' But scientific objectivity does not depend upon the psychology of the individual scientist; rather, it is the 'public character of science and its institutions which imposes a mental discipline upon the individual scientist, and which preserves the objectivity of science and its tradition of critically discussing new ideas' (Popper 1957/2005; 144). The idea that knowledge grows as a consequence of public debate among members of all disciplines and all fields ensures honesty and full disclosure among those involved. Popper's epistemology did not seek to demarcate a distinct scientific method, then, as no such thing really existed; rather, it provided a criterion for judging whether a particular theory or claim should be understood as capable of contributing to our understanding of the world (in any field, regardless of the subject-matter).

Pulling these various ideas together, then, we can see why Popper's conception of science (and of the growth of knowledge in general) was, and remains, so controversial. In place of the traditional view of science (as an *inductive* process which extrapolates *general laws* or hypotheses about the world from specific *observations*, and which have the capacity to *prove* that statements about facts are *true*), Popper suggested that science should be understood as a *deductive* process whereby theoretical solutions to *problems* are proposed and then falsified through critical discussion of the facts, or other theories. Hence, *unfalsifiable* theories are not scientific. No theory can be decisively *proven*, but they can be decisively *falsified*, hence, the scientist should not seek proofs, but rather falsifications, of scientific theories, through public engagement, debate, and empirical testing. Some theories will be easily falsified, others will not; however, it is the repeated and successive attempts to falsify existing theories and to replace them with others, which drives forward the process of scientific discovery, and increases our aggregate knowledge of the world. On this view, science becomes characterised as a trial and error process of conjecture and refutation. Individuals propose (often bold) theories about particular problems in the world, and in doing so invite others to falsify these theories. Scientific discovery requires the adoption of a critical attitude towards problems and their hypothetical solutions, and is born out of critical dialogue among a community of individuals:

> The advance of science is not due to the fact that more and more perceptual experiences accumulate in the course of time. Nor is it due to the fact that we are making ever better use of our senses. Out of uninterpreted sense-experiences science cannot be distilled, no matter how industriously we gather and sort them. Bold ideas, unjustified anticipations and speculative thought, are our only means for interpreting nature: . . . our only instrument for grasping her. (Popper, 1935/2007a; 280)

Scientific discovery is not clean and tidy; rather the history of science, 'like the history of all human ideas, is a history of irresponsible dreams, of obstinacy, and of error' (Popper 1963/2007b; 293). Rather than seek generalizable proofs of great and general *truths* through the bare application of reason, we should seek to remove *error* through a critical engagement with existing theories, ideas, traditions, and narratives, by testing them against what we ourselves have found out and what others have similarly thought and discovered. Understanding science as the accumulation of certain truths about the world 'hampers not only the boldness of our questions, but also the rigour and integrity of our tests. The wrong [or "traditional"] view of science betrays itself in the craving to be right; for it is not the *possession* of knowledge, of irrefutable truth, that makes the man of science, but his persistent, recklessly critical *quest* for truth' (Popper 1935/2007a; 281). His broad conclusion, then, was that we should 'give up on the idea of ultimate sources of knowledge, and admit that all knowledge is human; that it is mixed with our errors, our prejudices, our dreams, and our hopes; that all we can do is to grope for the truth even though it be beyond our reach' (Popper 1963/2007b; 39).

From science to social science

It is often thought that Popper developed a 'philosophy of science' and then applied this philosophy to the social sciences. But as we have already seen, Popper's aim was in fact slightly different. It was not merely to develop a philosophy of science: it was to provide a theory of epistemology which would explain, and contribute to, the process by which our knowledge of the world might grow, or, rather, it was to develop a theory about 'the development of human thought in *general* and of scientific thought in *particular*' (Popper 1963/2007b; 421). Hence, Popper did not seek to *apply* his 'philosophy of science' to society and politics; rather, he sought to provide a general explanation of the process by which understanding of the world might be gathered, which was *as true* of science as it was of social science or politics.

Broadly speaking, therefore, Popper believed that the growth of knowledge in the social sciences should be understood as progressing in roughly the same way – according to the same *logic* – as in the physical sciences. Social scientific inquiry should begin in the identification of social and political problems, and should seek to resolve these problems through a trial and error process of conjecture and refutation aimed at eliminating error in those theories and practices which currently exist, and in those hypothetical solutions offered by others. It is not the role of social theory to make generalizable and long-term prophecies about the future course of history, but – as it is in the physical sciences – to resolve specific problems in ways which might be criticized and tested by others, and to work out whether those solutions already in operation (and embodied in social and political institutions, and social practices) are the right ones. In the social sciences, as in the physical sciences, then, knowledge grows as a consequence of adopting a critical (a 'critical rationalist') attitude towards social and political problems and their hypothetical solutions, and engaging critically with others about existing theories and ideas.

Popper thus proposed that the physical and social sciences are characterized by a 'unity of method'. That is, he argued that 'all theoretical or generalizing sciences make use of the same method, whether they are natural or social sciences', namely, the trial and error process of conjecture and refutation of falsifiable hypotheses about existing problems, conducted among a community of individuals who have adopted a critical rationalist attitude towards existing ideas, theories, and practices (Popper 1957/2005; 120). Theories about society – about *social problems* – thus need to be falsifiable in the same way as do theories about problems commonly assumed to be in the province of the physical sciences. And just as Popper believed that falsifiability was the appropriate criterion for demarcating scientific from non-scientific theories in the physical sciences, so he believed that it did so also for social scientific theories, and theories in other fields too. In arguing as much, Popper believed that he was able to reveal the weakness (or, at least, the non-scientific character) of many theories which purport to be scientific (and hence, purport to add to human knowledge), but which do not. Three such theories were Adler's theory of 'individual psychology', Freud's theory of psychoanalysis, and Marxism. The problem with these theories, for Popper, was precisely that they were *unfalsifiable*: it was impossible to refute them. What impressed the Marxists, Freudians, and the Adlerians was, he argued, precisely the *explanatory power* of their theories, indeed, 'they appeared to be able to explain practically everything that happened within the fields to which they referred'. The study of them seemed to open

> your eyes to a new truth hidden from those not yet initiated. Once your eyes were thus opened you saw confirming instances everywhere: the world was full of *verifications* of the theory. Whatever happened always confirmed it. Thus its truth appeared manifest; and unbelievers were clearly people who did not want to see the manifest truth; who refused to see it, either because it was against their class interest, or because of their repressions which were still 'unanalysed' and crying out for treatment. (Popper 1963/2007b; 45)

We see in these theories, therefore, the error in taking verification by observation/experience as the demarcation between scientific theories and non-scientific theories (in the realms of the physical sciences, as well as the realms of the social sciences and psychology), and the folly of (inductively) extrapolating theories from facts: namely that the facts can often prove anything that the theorist likes, and hence they prove nothing. What made the theories of individuals like Copernicus, Kepler, and Galileo important *scientific* theories, Popper believed, was that they could be shown to be *false*. Even Newton's theory of universal gravitation and dynamics was *falsifiable*, as was shown by Einstein. But even Einstein could not have falsified Freud's theory of psychoanalysis or Adler's 'individual psychology' or Marxism because no appeal to the facts or rival theories could ever undermine them. Any patient of Freudian psychoanalysis who felt that their behaviour could not be explained by some combination of repressed urges of one kind or another was merely considered 'in denial' and in need of further treatment. Similarly, any member of a capitalist society who rejected the class struggle or the inevitable emergence of communism was merely suffering from 'false consciousness' and in need of further education in Marxist dogma.

We might recall (from Chapter 1) that Popper believed it was precisely this unwillingness among Austrian Marxists in the 1930s to accept what was going on around them, and their desire to understand all events and historical developments as confirmations of their theory (rather than challenges to it) which led to their collapse in the face of rising fascism. Marxists of that time saw not *refutations*, but *verifications*, of their ideals in the events which were transpiring in Vienna and, hence, did not possess the theoretical resources necessary to identify their errors until it was too late, and fascism had triumphed. However, Popper believed that the fault lay not with the Austrian Marxists as such, but with the doctrine of Marxism itself. Marxism was unfalsifiable (and hence, not a theory which could contribute to human knowledge), because it was a *historicist* doctrine. It is important to understand Popper's critique of historicism in detail, as it is fundamental to his ideas about the appropriate conduct of the social sciences and the practice of politics.

Popper described historicism as, broadly speaking, 'the doctrine that history is controlled by specific historical or evolutionary laws whose discovery would allow us to prophesy the destiny of man' (Popper 1945/2006a; 4). It therefore embodies the view that 'a truly scientific or philosophical attitude towards politics, and a deeper understanding of social life in general, must be based upon a contemplation and interpretation of human history' (Popper 1945/2006a; 3). It is, he said, an 'approach to the social sciences which assumes that historical prediction is their principal aim, and which assumes that this aim is attainable by discovering the "rhythms" or "patterns", the "laws" or the "trends" which underlie the development of history' (Popper 1957/2005; 3). Historicism, then, is an approach to understanding society and politics by understanding social and political phenomena as products of historical forces; as things which have *origins*, which are thought to develop towards their own internally defined endpoints or goals, and which exist in their current form as the culmination of historical events. Consequently, the study of social and political institutions, norms, and conventions cannot be undertaken in abstraction from the historical forces and conditions which brought them into the world. The study of politics and society is, on this view, little more or less than the study of *history*.

This view, Popper believed, was a popular and pernicious one, in human history, the history of political thought, and in what passed for social and political discourse at the time. Some of the oldest and most obvious examples of historicism, he thought, were those religions which identify a 'chosen people' whose role is to function as 'the selected instrument of [God's] will', and who, in assuming this role correctly, 'will inherit the Earth' (Popper, 1945/2006a; 4). In such doctrines, the laws of historical development are laid down by the will of God, and it is the role of the chosen people to do what they can to hasten the inevitable coming to fruition of the prophecies foretold in their holy texts. Religious and secular forms of historicism thus share the same broad features, Popper argued: they are collectivist, in the sense that they speak in terms of groups rather than individuals (they speak, for example, of 'peoples' or 'nations' or 'races' or 'classes'), and the ends they prophesize are always distant and remote. For although we may have a good idea of what we are striving for, 'we will have to go a long way before we reach it. And the way is not only long, but winding, leading up and down, right and left. Accordingly, it will be possible to bring every conceivable historical event well within the scheme of interpretation' (Popper 1945/2006a; 5). Like the claims of the Freudian psychoanalyst, the Adlerian psychologist, and the Marxist, then, religious doctrines which foretell the destiny of a chosen people are unfalsifiable, and hence, cannot contribute to human knowledge.

Popper believed that the history of the social and political sciences was littered with thinkers who had adopted the historicist approach. Thinkers with philosophical and political conclusions as diverse as Plato, Hegel, Rousseau, Mill, and Comte were nevertheless united with Marx in embracing the historicist method – indeed, he believed, Marx was merely the most recent and persuasive advocate of historicism. For Marx, of course, the 'chosen people' or 'group' was the working class, and the historical laws were not laid down by God but by economic forces. And for Hegel, the 'chosen people' was 'the nation', and the laws of historical development described the dialectical progression of the nation (understood as the embodiment of the Spirit) towards freedom, or self-realization. The view that Marx and Hegel (and, consequently, Marxists and Hegelians) shared with other historicist thinkers, then, was that human societies are products of impersonal and overarching laws of historical development, and that this fact determined the appropriate conduct of the social sciences, and the appropriate character of politics. It also allowed those capable of knowing the laws of history to predict the future of humankind. The point of the *social sciences*, for the historicist, was to reveal those historical laws of development which determine the nature and content of society (and hence, our social relations with one another, our social attitudes, and the implicit social norms which govern and regulate our lives) at any given time. The point of *politics* – and the correct role and responsibility of political institutions like the state – was primarily to set the conditions appropriate for the realization of those goals or ends determined by the historical laws of development. Popper developed his own approach to social science out of an engagement with historicist ideas. Therefore, for the remainder of this section, I will discuss the implications of the historicist approach for the study of *society* (and Popper's critique of it), before going on to discuss its *political* implications in the next section.

I have already mentioned that, for Popper, historicism is characterized primarily by the claim that it is the appropriate role of the social scientist to seek those *historical* laws which determine the nature and content of society and, hence, that sociology is little more or less than the study of *theoretical history*. Historicism thus embodies a fundamental rejection of the idea that the methods of the natural and physical sciences can be unproblematically employed in the social sciences. Historicists argue that the methods of the physical sciences cannot hope to yield insights into social and political life, for four principal reasons.

First, historicists reject the idea that it is possible to infer generalizable, immutable laws governing social and political life in the way that natural scientists believe it is possible in the physical sciences. The overarching aim of the physical scientist, historicists claim, is to derive general laws governing the structure of the universe, and the behaviour of physical elements, which are not rooted in any particular historical period and which are, therefore, considered timeless. 'Physical laws, or the "laws of nature," [the physical sciences tell us], are valid anywhere and always; for the physical world is ruled by a system of physical uniformities invariable throughout space and time. Sociological laws, however, or the "the laws of social life" differ in different places and periods' (Popper, 1957/2005; 4). While the historicist might concede that there are certain trivial regularities that it is possible to identify in the character of social life which might extend beyond any one particular historical period, they hold that it is not possible to identify more substantive (and therefore, useful) laws which stand independent of the historical period in which they are observed. 'A method which ignores this limitation and attempts a generalization of social uniformities will, according to historicism, implicitly assume that the regularities in question are everlasting' (Popper 1957/2005; 5). Such a theory will deny that 'society ever develops; or that it ever changes significantly; or that social developments, if there are any, can affect the basic regularities of social life' (Popper, 1957/ 2005; 5–6). Historicists therefore argue that instead of adopting the 'methodologically naïve' view that we can simply import the methods of the physical sciences into the study of politics and society, we should take seriously the *historically rooted* nature of social relations. Thus, for example, Marxists like Karl Mannheim, and critical theorists like Habermas, Adorno, and Horkheimer, all followed Marx himself in claiming that the study of society needed to be primarily a process of analysing the particular social relations characteristic of any particular epoch (and their emergence) rather than one of deriving universal laws of social life which are true for all time and for all epochs. Similarly, the idealism of Hegel and his more recent supporters – so vehemently opposed by the logical positivists as well as Popper – embodied a rejection of the notion that 'truth' could be discovered via science, claiming instead that truth was itself a historical phenomenon which could only be revealed via an engagement with those historical laws from which it emerged. To understand society, these and other historicists argued, we must approach the study of social relations as historical phenomena – produced by historical forces, shaped by historical circumstances, and understandable as products of history itself, rather than as things which can be rendered intelligible in abstraction from their origins. Importantly, we should take seriously the importance of *culture*, and the ability of human beings to shape the future of the society in which they live. Historicism holds that the search for timeless social laws leaves no room for *activism*, that is, the possibility that individual members of society might, through conscious will or accident, shape their own future and the future of their society. Innovation and creativity only exist within – and are defined by – the general structure of overarching laws which govern social life for all time and it is therefore these laws, not human beings themselves, which determine the character of social and political life, and the course of social change.

Now this may sound confusing, given that we have already suggested that it is characteristic of historicism that its defenders *do* seek overarching laws of history. It is important, therefore, to re-affirm that, for Popper, the aim of historicism is not to discover the laws of any one particular historical period and then to assert that these laws must hold for all historical periods; rather, it is to discover those more general laws which determine the *transition* from one historical period to another. That is, historicism seeks laws of *historical development.* For example, a social scientist may look at contemporary capitalist society and identify certain laws which hold within it (e.g. the law that increased demand for a scarce resource raises the market value of that resource). This will be a law which holds true in capitalist societies, but it may well not hold true in societies (in history or in other parts of the world) which order their economies differently: for example, feudal societies or planned economies. Hence, it is not possible to speak of universal, trans-historical laws of the kind mentioned above, because these laws will only hold in certain societies at certain times. We cannot speak meaningfully of, say, laws of economics which extend across all historical periods; rather, we can only speak of the laws of economics of the capitalist period, or the economics of the feudal period, and so on. What the historicist seeks, therefore, is not the extrapolation of generalizable, trans-historical laws of social behaviour from specific observations of one particular period, but the deeper laws which determine how, when, and why one historical period becomes another. What rendered Marx's theory of historical materialism so powerful and radical, for example, was not that it merely identified the past existence of distinct historical epochs, each characterized by their own social, economic, and political norms and institutions, but that it also provided an overarching explanation of how and why each period gave way to the next and, hence, how the present system would give way to further epochs in the future. Similarly, Hegel's dialectical conception of history did not merely delineate those historical epochs that had already existed, it provided a means of predicting how history would develop in the future, and the ends to which history itself was inevitably headed. And, Popper believed, we can find similar claims in the work of Plato, Comte, Mill, Rousseau, and all those other historicists who have written on the social sciences: common to all of them, he argued, was the idea that the role of sociology was to derive general laws or 'uniformities' in history which could explain the development of successive historical periods and, hence, the *origins* of each set of social relations which characterize them.

A *second*, and intimately connected, criticism that historicists make of adopting the methods of the natural sciences in the study of society is that the principal means of obtaining reliable knowledge in the physical sciences is wholly inappropriate in a social and political context. Physical scientists infer general laws through an observation of the behaviour of physical elements. They introduce 'artificial controls, artificial isolation, and thereby [ensure] the reproduction of similar conditions, and the consequent production of certain effects' (Popper, 1957/2005; 7). The idea that it is possible to observe social and political phenomena in this way and derive general laws from these observations which exist for all time is absurd, they believe. This is because the structure of inference that works in the physical sciences breaks down in a social and political context. In the physical sciences, it is possible to observe certain behaviours and to infer from this that under the same conditions the same elements/processes would behave/occur in the same way. Hence, it is an important aim for the physical scientist to stipulate and then isolate the specific conditions necessary to test specific behaviours and hypotheses. That is, she conducts experiments aimed at providing specific answers to specific questions which can then provide a basis for a general law. Historicists argue, however, that no such inferential relationship can exist when studying society. Popper illustrated this historicist contention with reference to Mannheim's *Man and Society* but, it becomes clear in his later war of words with Habermas and Adorno during the 'positivism debate' in the 1960s, he also identified it as a belief shared by critical theorists. It is not possible to isolate social and political phenomena in the way that it is possible to isolate physical elements, the claim goes, and so 'social experiments' will always produce indeterminate results. Furthermore, he argued that historicists like Mannheim, Adorno, and Habermas held that any social experiments must be necessarily radical and holistic. The components of society cannot be broken down and examined in isolation, and hence, social experiments should not seek to do so. The subject-matter of the social sciences (i.e. people) is too complex and too changeable to be compatible with the physical sciences' need for objectivity, control, and the dispassionate isolation of individuated subjects. So observation and experimentation, while perfectly valid and intelligible with regard to the gathering of knowledge in the physical sciences, cannot provide the *social* scientist with the unambiguous, objective knowledge that they would need in order to infer generalizable laws for all time and for all people. Also, as we mentioned earlier, historicism holds that the inference that 'in similar circumstances, similar things will happen' is only really applicable within particular historical periods. Cultures change and ideas develop; as a consequence, each new historical period may well represent a genuinely new system of relations, ideas, and assumptions of a like that has never been seen before. Consequently, there are no observable, transhistorical 'similar circumstances' in the past which one might look to in order to make sense of the present or the future. As Popper put it, in a

> world described by physics nothing can happen that is truly and intrinsically new. An engine may be invented, but we can always analyse it as a rearrangement of elements which are anything but new. Newness in physics is merely the newness of arrangements or combinations. In direct opposition to this, social newness [for the historicist] is an intrinsic form of newness . . . For in social life, the same old factors in a new arrangement are never really the same old factors . . . This is held [by historicists] to be significant for the consideration of the development of new stages or periods in history, each of which differs intrinsically from the other. (Popper, 1957/2005; 9)

There is no more important a moment in the study of social life for the historicist than the birth of a genuinely new period of history. And historicists believe that the methods of the physical sciences hold no key to understanding such a change, or even rendering such a change intelligible.

A *third*, and related, feature of historicism is its *holism*. The methods of the physical sciences are, historicists claim, *atomistic*: they study particular elements in particular circumstances. They are also *ahistorical* in the sense that they do not examine the historical characteristics of the object in question, but merely its behaviour under certain conditions. This approach is entirely appropriate to the physical sciences, they argue. Although it may be interesting to explore, say, the history of the solar system, it is not necessary to do so in order to understand its present state. This is because its present state is 'independent of the history of the system. The structure of the system, its future movements and developments, are fully determined by the present constellation of its members . . . [T]he history of the structure, although it may be interesting, contributes nothing to our understanding of its behaviour, of its mechanism, or its future development' (Popper, 1957/2005; 16). Social groups, however, are very different. Historicists believe that social groups should never be understood as mere aggregates of persons. Social groups are more than the mere sum of their total members, and more also than the sum total of personal relationships which exist among its members at any one time. For historicists like Mannheim, it is crucial to understand that 'all social groups have their own traditions, their own institutions, their own rites. Historicism claims that we must study the history of the group, its traditions, and institutions, if we wish to understand and explain it as it is now, and if we wish to understand and perhaps explain its future development' (Popper, 1957/2005; 16). Again, therefore, we note the historicist idea that to understand society, we must understand the *history* of the *group*. This is why, for the historicist, sociology is merely a form of theoretical history: to understand social life in any particular historical period, it is necessary to examine the overall character of the social group as a whole, and its historical origins. One should not merely examine the individuals which constitute this group at any one time; one should instead take as the subject the internal dynamics and character of the group *as a whole*.

Fourthly, Popper claimed that historicists throughout history, from Plato to Comte, Rousseau, Marx, and Habermas, were united in their claim that social scientists should adopt a *methodologically essentialist,* rather than a *methodologically nominalist,* approach to understanding society. Popper's rejection of essentialism was noted in the section above regarding his claims concerning the folly in seeking the 'essence' of particular academic disciplines in the interests if splitting them off from one another. However, these terms need further explanation in the current context. Popper understood methodological essentialism as an approach to science founded by Aristotle, which states that in order to explain something one must 'penetrate its essence'. 'Methodological essentialists', Popper argued, 'are inclined to formulate scientific questions in such terms as "what is matter?" or "what is force?" or "what is justice?", [or, as in the discussion earlier about disciplines, "what is philosophy?" or "what is science?"] and they believe that a penetrating answer to such questions, revealing the real or essential meaning of these terms, and thereby the real or true nature of the essences denoted by them, is at least a necessary prerequisite of scientific research, if not its main task' (Popper, 1957/2005; 25). Methodological nominalists, on the other hand, seek no such fundamental answers. Rather, they frame their questions in terms of how things behave under certain conditions. From what we have already discussed, it is clear that historicists impute a methodological nominalism to the physical sciences, and with good reason. There is indeed a strong trend of methodological nominalism in the physical sciences. Physics, for example, does not attempt to define the 'essence' of light or gravity, rather, it observes how these things behave in certain conditions. Historicists believe that this is inadequate for the study of society and that, in order to understand social life, we must understand its internal dynamics, its structure, its history, and its origins. We must therefore do more than merely observe the behaviour of its members; we must get under its skin, and go beyond a mere description of its surface behaviour. We must seek its *essence.* We need to get to grips with the group's culture, and the way in which this culture has developed throughout history.

Considered together, then, these four characteristic features of historicism provide a general methodology for the social sciences which stands utterly opposed to that defended by Popper. It is *essentialist* and *holistic*, in the sense that social scientists should seek to understand the essential nature of the social group as a whole, rather than the *particular* relations or interactions that occur among *individual* members of that society. It collapses the distinction between the study of society and the study of the *history* of society; to study society is simply to study its history and no more. And, despite rejecting the naturalistic conceit that it is possible to establish generalizable social laws from observed behaviour within particular historical periods, historicists nevertheless cling to the worst aspects of the inductive method in claiming that it is possible to reveal overarching laws of historical development which can *prophesize* the long-term future of society history, and the fate of humankind. Popper thus identified both anti-naturalistic and pro-naturalistic doctrines in historicism: historicists rejected the methodological nominalism, atomism, ahistoricism, and the primacy of observation and experiment which they saw in the methods of the physical sciences, but crucially retained other aspects of the natural scientific method which suited their purposes: primarily, the idea that the social sciences could and should infer general social (i.e. historical) laws capable of predicting long-term future events.

Popper pointed out, however, what many readers will already have noticed: that all the historicists' criticisms of the scientific method are in fact criticisms of the traditional, inductive view of science that Popper sought to undermine. They represent a critique of what we might call 'scientism' in social theory. Consequently, their general position (that it was not appropriate to use the methods of the physical sciences in the social sciences) was, for Popper, premised upon a fundamental misunderstanding of science and, hence, what it would *mean* to adopt the scientific method in the study of society. The problem with the historicists, for Popper, was not that they believed that the inductive model was inappropriate to the study of society (indeed, Popper agreed with this claim), but that they drew the wrong lessons from this point, and proposed a mistaken alternative to it. Their claim, remember, was that the inductive method is indeed appropriate for the study of physical and natural phenomena, but that it is not appropriate for the study of social phenomena. They, like the logical positivists and others, were therefore in the business of drawing boundaries between disciplines on the basis of their various subject-matters, and the methodologies appropriate to each, in ways which were anathema to Popper. The historicists accepted unquestioningly the supremacy of the inductive method in the physical sciences; their claim was that natural scientists should do their thing, and social scientists should do theirs. Popper, of course, disagreed. He argued that the inductive model did not represent an appropriate method by which to study society, but only because he thought that the inductive model did not represent an appropriate method by which to study *anything*. He thus agreed with the historicists that social scientists should abandon the inductive model, not so that they could replace it with historicism, but so that they could replace it with a more coherent conception of science and the scientific method.

In place of historicism and scientism, Popper defended a conception of the social sciences built around his conception of critical rationalism, that is, one rooted firmly in his wider epistemological ideas which emphasised the clash of ideas, the fallibility of reason, and the gradual step-by-step reform of social and political life on the basis of rigorous testing, critique, and debate. Its characteristic elements stand opposed to historicism, and are thus:

(1) The principal purpose of the social sciences is to identify and attempt to resolve social problems by proposing theories about them, and subjecting these and other theories to a rigorous process of refutation and testing, in circumstances

of epistemological uncertainty. It is not the role of the social scientist to make long-term, general *prophecies* about the future historical development of society, or to justify social and political reform by appealing to unfalsifiable social and historical laws, or to reveal the 'end of history' as Marx, Hegel, and others did. Because there are no laws of historical development which can be inferred from specific observations, social scientists cannot make predictions above and beyond what is supported by the sum total of knowledge already in existence. They must base their predictions and theories on the information available, because that is all there is. Human actions will often lead to unexpected outcomes. Social reforms initiated in good faith will have unintended consequences. Political activity will lead to unforeseen events and unpredictable conclusions. Consequently, the 'main task of the theoretical social sciences' is not to prophesize the future of human development, but to 'trace the unintended social repercussions of intentional human actions' (Popper, 1963/2007b; 460). Social life is 'not only a trial of strength among opposing groups [like classes or nations]: it is action within a more or less resilient or brittle framework of institutions and traditions, and it creates . . . many unforeseen reactions in the framework, some of them may even be unforeseeable (Popper, 1945/2006b; 105). Consequently, predictions in the social sciences, like predictions in the physical sciences, should only be short-term, limited, and falsifiable; *prophecies* of the kind indulged in by historicists are none of these things, and so are unscientific and cannot represent contributions to knowledge.

(2) The appropriate objects of social enquiry are not laws of history or social groups, as Marxists, Hegelians, and other historicists contend, but observable social institutions and arrangements, and the actions and interactions of *individual human beings*. The social sciences should thus be 'methodologically *individualist*' rather than 'methodologically

holistic'. Society should be understood as an aggregate of *individuals*, and the actions of *individuals* within this system should be understood to count. Historicism subordinates the individual to society: it is interested not in the specific actions of individual human actors, but in the general social laws governing the actions of all members of society at any one time. Far from emphasizing the capacity of individuals to shape society according to their own collective will, as is their professed intention, the historicists present a conception of society in which the actions and thoughts of individual human beings are stifled by history and determined by historical forces over which they have no control, and from which they are powerless to escape. Historicists thus fall into the same trap as those inductivists who believe that it is possible to infer generalizable laws in the study of human societies.

(3) The social sciences have an important practical function: through the endeavours of individual social scientists, who have adopted the appropriate critical rationalist attitude towards social problems and the theories in common currency in social scientific discourse, and who have engaged in critical discussion and debate with others about these matters, it is possible to furnish legislators with the theories they need to reform society in a way that is humane, just, and compatible with individual freedom. Social science provides a guide for social reform. Reforms must be short-term, gradual, and *piecemeal*, rather than long-term, radical, and *utopian*, for all the reasons mentioned in point 1, above. Instead of trying to resolve all the problems of society in one fell swoop by appealing to some overarching plan rooted in revealed knowledge about the true nature or purpose of social and political institutions, social scientists should identify specific problems and seek to resolve them through a process of conjecture and refutation. By engaging in such a process, problems might be identified, examined,

and resolved in a *piecemeal* fashion, as theories are proposed, debated, tested, and, perhaps, rejected in a constant search for error. It is thus the principal role of social scientists to determine the purpose of existing social and political institutions, to evaluate whether they are successfully achieving their purpose, and, if they are not, to propose new and bold alternative arrangements.

(4) The social sciences should be 'methodologically *nominalist*' rather than 'methodologically *essentialist*'. It is not the role of the social scientist to trace the historical origins of particular social relations, or to grasp the *essence* of a particular society, but to identify genuine social problems and work out how they might be resolved. According to Popper's wider epistemology, the purpose, legitimacy and effectiveness of existing social institutions (and the theories justifying and explaining them) are inevitably conjectural; the role of the government or some other social institution may change in response to wider changes in our understanding of the world and individual members of society and, hence, no institution or arrangement is set in stone as legitimate for all time. Similarly, no particular set of social institutions might appropriately claim its legitimacy in some projected future goal for all humanity: arguments in favour of particular arrangements and institutions (and, hence, these arrangements and institutions themselves) must remain conjectural, and may be falsified by empirical or theoretical challenges. The aim of the social sciences is thus not to build grand theories about the nature of society and politics, or to search for the origins of social relations, and it is not to seek certain and irrefutable *truths* about the nature of society and its development, but to eliminate *error* in those theories about society and politics which have been proposed by testing them against the sum total of all the knowledge (derived from all the various 'disciplines') that bear upon that issue.

In summary, then, we can see that Popper's vision of the social sciences was rooted firmly in his wider views about epistemology: knowledge in the sciences, the social sciences, and elsewhere, grows in the same way and according to the same logic. Popper shared with the historicists the view that the inductive model was inappropriate for the study of society, but fundamentally disagreed with their alternative. He saw the historicists as seeking a new form of social inquiry concerned primarily with foretelling the future of humanity by identifying laws of history (which determined the nature and appropriate structure of social relations, and the actions of those individuals within it) and examining the culture of society as a whole, in order that they might structure society according to a fixed plan or blueprint. Popper, on the other hand, believed that both the historicist and inductive approaches should be replaced with his own approach which emphasized trial and error, conjecture and refutation, and piecemeal social reform guided by the elimination of error in existing theories about society and its problems. In social science, then, as in the physical sciences, the driving thought for Popper was that we can learn from our mistakes. By identifying problems, proposing solutions, and debating these problems critically with others who are as ready to listen to rational arguments as we are, we can identify the incoherences and falsehoods in existing theories just as we can identify failures in existing practices and institutions, and in doing so we can work out how best to identify and resolve social problems through a process of piecemeal social reform.

From social science to politics

Popper's views about the appropriate role and responsibilities of social and political institutions represent an inversion of the historicist position, and a rejection of all the normative, epistemological, and methodological foundations upon which it is built. The aim of the historicist, remember, was to study society in such a way as to reveal those historical laws of development which determined its nature and shape. Having done so, historicists could consult these underlying historical laws in order to infer the future development of society. Once sufficient knowledge of society had been gained – knowledge, that is, of its culture, its underlying history, and the complex web of subjective interactions and assumptions which combine to create the social whole – it was possible for the historicist to work out not only how society had got to where it had, but where it was heading. The historical laws of development therefore provided historicists not only with the key to understanding the past, but the tools necessary to prophesize the future. By appealing to past examples and events, and by understanding the nature of human beings and the particular social and historical context in which they live, historicists held that it was possible to predict with relative certainty the outcome of political proposals and decisions. Furthermore, having identified what brings new social and historical periods into being – that is, what social, political, economic, and legal conditions need to hold in order for society to move from one period to another – historicists felt able to use this knowledge as an appropriate justification for social and political reform. Once one understands that society develops according to objective historical laws, and that history requires certain conditions to be in place in order for society to move to the next stage, then it becomes straightforwardly obvious that social, economic, and political change should be geared towards the bringing about of those conditions conducive to either ushering in the new era, or protecting society from such change. Social reform is thus viewed by historicists as a tool by which society might either be made ready for the birth of a new era, or protected from moving into this new, and worse, state of affairs.

Importantly, then, Popper believed that historicist politics was fundamentally *utopian* and *elitist*. It was *utopian* in the sense that historicist social science is not merely a passive process of understanding and interpreting the laws of history; it is both *active* and *purposive*: it embodies a desire to discover not just what society looked like in the past, but where it is heading and, importantly, where it *should* be heading, and how it might get there. Historicism therefore demands that 'we must determine our ultimate political aim, or the Ideal State, before taking any practical action. Only when this ultimate aim is determined, in rough outline at least, only when we are in possession of something like a blueprint of the society at which we aim, only then can we consider the best ways and means for its realization, and to draw up a plan for rational action' (Popper, 1945/2006a; 167). Social engineering, or the process of social reform with a view to solving social and political problems, is thus a *holistic* and *collectivist* endeavour: it aims at nothing less than the wholesale restructuring of society in order that it might bring about, or protect, an idealized form of politics in line with historical laws. A utopian form of social engineering holds that we need to know the ends or goals to which we strive before engaging in social reform: it would be *irrational* for us to implement a policy or set of reforms without first knowing why we are doing so, and what we wanted that policy to achieve. We thus work out what kind of society and politics we want to have, and then do those things (determined by the historical laws of development) which help to bring that society and politics about.

Utopian social engineering thus 'recommends the reconstruction of society as a whole' with the aim of bringing about radical and very long-term changes in our social and political arrangements, in line with a distant idealized conception of how we should all live and what society should look like. But, Popper argued, such a view is rendered incoherent by the fact that we cannot predict with certainty the outcome of our actions or decisions in the way that the historicists believe we can. This, again, is because reason is fallible: we may think we can provide a successful plan for the achievement of some future society, and that we can foresee all potential problems along the way, but we cannot. The practical and long-term consequences of our decisions are, as we saw in point (1) in the previous section, 'hard to calculate, owing to our limited experiences'.

Historicism 'claims to plan rationally for the whole of society,' but 'we do not possess anything like the factual knowledge which would be necessary to make good such an ambitious claim. We cannot possess such knowledge since we have insufficient practical experience in this kind of planning, and knowledge of facts must be based on experience. At present, the sociological knowledge necessary for large-scale engineering is simply non-existent' (Popper, 1945/2006a; 171). The idea that we can (and should) *plan* what a society should look like in advance and then implement social reforms in accordance with this plan, is a fallacy, Popper believed. 'Only a minority of social institutions are consciously designed, while the vast majority have "grown" as the undesigned results of human actions . . . [and] most of the few institutions which were consciously and successfully designed . . . do not turn out according to plan . . . because of the unintended social repercussions resulting from the intentional creation' (Popper, 1945/2006b; 103). Hence, as we mentioned in the previous section, it should not be considered an important role of the social sciences to understand society such that its future can be rationally planned and predicted; rather, given that this process is ultimately doomed to failure, it should 'study the unwieldiness, the resilience or the brittleness of the social stuff, of its resistance to our attempts to mould it and work with it' (Popper, 1945/2006b; 104). The reason we cannot predict with certainty the outcome of our decisions, or what long-term social and political conditions we should aim for, is precisely because it is impossible for us to infer such things from present circumstances or events. The reason we cannot plan the future in response to the past, and the reason we cannot justify social and political reform by appealing to the an idealized future (attainable via a proper grasp of the historical laws of development) is because such an approach would require the adoption of an *inductivist* method which Popper believes is mistaken and incoherent: it requires too much of reason. The best we can do given the problem of induction, and the inability of reason to provide absolutely certain knowledge of the long-term future consequences of our actions and initiatives, he believed, is to admit that utopianism cannot provide the blueprints or the certainty that historicists require, and adopt instead his idea of *piecemeal social engineering* in its place, which does not require the inductive inference of historical laws, but which is rooted instead in our experience of the world – limited and short-term as it is – and is consistent with his wider epistemological ideas about the growth of knowledge.

We will discuss piecemeal engineering in more detail a little later in this and the next chapter. Before doing so, it is important to deal with Popper's second critique of historicist politics: that it is *elitist.* Popper felt that the historicist approach to politics was *elitist* in the sense that it presupposed that power should lie in the hands of those who could see and understand the laws of development and, hence, who could know the future of humankind, the inevitable outcome of social and political decisions, and how best to establish the Ideal State. It was thus, Popper believed, a vindication of centralized planning, and the coalescence of power in the hands of those who possessed the requisite knowledge to implement social and political reforms in ways which would bring about the creation of new historical periods. This argument, he said, has been used by dictators and tyrants throughout the ages to ignore the expressed wishes of the people, to oppress them, to brutalize them, and to claim that they were only doing so for their own good, and in pursuit of a goal that only the tyrant could see or understand. We see in this claim the earlier point that historicism embodies the notion of a 'chosen people'. Popper believed that it was characteristic of all forms of historicism that knowledge of history (and hence, what needed to be done in order to make sure history progressed in the right way) did not belong to everyone, but to a few. And as political power should rightfully belong only to those who possess this knowledge it followed that historicism represented an argument for the consolidation of power in the few, and provided the justification for this few to do whatever they wanted to do, all the while claiming that their actions were justified by the goals that only they could understand, and that their views and ideas were right even if others refused to agree.

Furthermore, Popper believed that the elitism and utopianism at the heart of historicist politics conspired to silence free expression, thought, and any criticism of those in charge. The reason for this, he said, was that the kind of long-term, large-scale, profound social reforms which were the stuff of historicist politics would 'cause considerable inconvenience to many, and for a considerable span of time. Accordingly, the Utopian engineer will have to be deaf to many complaints; in fact, it will be part of his business to suppress unreasonable objections . . . But with it, he must invariably suppress reasonable criticism also' (Popper, 1945/2006a; 169). Those with access to the privileged information contained in history are not only able to determine what should and should not be done, they also possess the power to determine what is reasonable and unreasonable criticism. Without access to this privileged information, the ignorant majority have little or no grounds on which to criticize the actions of their rulers, to engage in meaningful debate about the appropriate ends of social and political institutions, or to judge the legitimacy or illegitimacy of those who rule them. They simply do not possess the requisite knowledge to make such judgments or to engage meaningfully in debates about what the state should do, or the goals to which it should be committed.

Historicism is thus, for Popper, *epistemologically* mistaken, and *normatively* objectionable: it is premised upon the false *epistemological* assumption that it is possible to infer historical laws of development, and it is *normatively* objectionable in the sense that it appeals to these historical laws in order to justify the oppression of the general population by leaders who, and who alone, are privy to their secrets. Moreover, given that any goals to which the ruling elite are committed are necessarily long-term and, hence, unlikely to be achieved in the lifetime of the present ruler or dictator, it is crucial that successors to the dictator are *appointed* rather than *elected*. Holding free and fair elections, and allowing the people to decide who rules them, may well result in the election of a ruler who does not, and cannot, possess the requisite knowledge to govern in a way that brings about the Ideal State. Hence, democratic elections – and with them any notion of popular sovereignty or accountability – are rejected in favour of a system which allows the ruling elite to appoint their successors and, hence, to perpetuate its unassailable dominance over the people across generations.

Popper thus believed that historicism provided the philosophical justification for *totalitarianism* in that it placed ultimate and unchecked power in the hands of a ruling elite that need not justify itself to anyone for any reason. It rendered democratic politics impossible by denying the people the requisite resources they needed to form their own political judgments and the requisite democratic institutions or mechanisms necessary for them to elect or remove from power those who ruled them. It took away the ability of the people to criticize their rulers. And, importantly it subordinated the good of the individual to the good of society as a whole. All these things find their modern expression in Nazism, Fascism and Communism, and hence, he argued that historicism has provided the normative and philosophical foundation for some of the most heinous and oppressive regimes in the history of the world. These are, of course, powerful claims. But what rendered them even more powerful, however, and what made *The Open Society and Its Enemies* such an explosive and controversial book, was that having argued that the seeds of modern *totalitarianism* lie in *historicism*, he then argued that the seeds of *historicism* lie in the work of some of the most revered and celebrated figures in history. Thus it was that Popper laid the blame for the rise of modern totalitarianism at the door of a diverse range of thinkers who had, up to that point, been acknowledged to be some of the most important and humane voices in the development of Western social and political thought. So how did he come to such a conclusion?

Although he identified historicist tendencies in Mill, Comte, and Rousseau, Popper spent the majority of *The Open Society* tracing the development of historicism – and hence, modern totalitarianism – through the work of Plato, Hegel, and Marx. Its earliest incarnation, he argued, was in the philosophy of ancient Greece, in particular the ideas of Hesiod, who 'made use of the idea of a general trend or tendency in historical development' (Popper, 1945/2006a; 7). This tendency, he believed, was one of physical and moral degeneration. He identified it, too, in the work of another Greek philosopher, Heraclitus, who claimed that the world was not *static* (as was the dominant view at the time) but rather characterized by constant *change*. Importantly, Heraclitus's view of history and change contained within it an important idea that would come to characterize all later historicist thought – that the world was not only in a constant state of change but that this change proceeds according to some 'inexorable and inevitable *law of destiny*' (Popper, 1945/2006a; 10).

For Popper, this view was most fully and obviously expressed by Plato. Popper believed that Plato's vision of the world embodied elements from both Hesiod and Heraclitus, in that he held that the world is characterized by change, and that, moreover, this change brings with it moral and physical degeneration. Societies are not static, Plato believed. They change, and in changing they tend towards decay and corruption. Therefore, he held that the principal role of a just state is to arrest all change and, hence, to protect the polity from descending into corruption. In a long and impassioned deconstruction of Plato's claims concerning justice and the qualities which characterise just and legitimate leaders, Popper argued that Plato's entire political vision was aimed at halting the development of history and maintaining stability and unity at virtually any cost. The key to understanding this, Popper claimed, was Plato's theory of the Forms. Plato believed that all existing earthly phenomena had an ideal Form which could not be truly or completely achieved in the real world. Any existing physical object is merely the flawed physical embodiment of the Form of these things, which existed in some idealized past. Consequently, any existing *state* would be merely an imperfect copy of the Form of the state, existing in an idealised and pristine past. Therefore, for Plato, the historical development of all things is little more than their continued journey *away* from their ideal and perfect Form (in the past) *towards* a more corrupted and flawed version.

Popper continued that, for Plato, the just state is one characterized primarily by unity and peace. The Form of the state is unified and harmonious, and unthreatened by vested interest or conflict. The Form of the ruling regime is one which can secure this unity for all its members. Hence, the just state is one which is as unified and harmonious as possible, as unthreatened by internal conflicts as it can be, and governed by political leaders who have the requisite strength and knowledge to do what is necessary to secure social and political conditions which are as much like their Forms as possible: perfect, unified, and unchanging. Plato is clear that the worst fate that can befall any society is that it allows any room for disunity. So much is proven in his sketch of the history of the state, in which he claims (in a move thought by Popper to be characteristic of all historicists) to have identified a series of distinct social and political periods which, for Plato, were brought about by the introduction of unharmonious tendencies and disunifying events into the otherwise harmonious state. Plato believed that the most just state was that of a *Kingship*, in which political power was held by the 'wisest and most god-like of men' (Popper, 1945/2006a; 40). However, without careful protection, such a state inevitably descends into *Timocracy* – the rule of the nobles who seek honour and fame – as a result of individual ambition and greed for power. As some members of society become envious of those with power, they seek to gain power and distinction through the acquisition of economic and social resources: ability to rule becomes associated less with wisdom and more with wealth, until, after some time, Timocracy collapses into *Oligarchy*, whereby the rich pass a law which 'disqualifies from public office all those whose means do not reach the stipulated amount' (Popper, 1945/2006a; 42). Oligarchy in turn exacerbates conflicts and enmities between the rich and the poor until, finally, civil war breaks out between the two classes. The poor, greater in number than the rich, overthrow their rich oppressors and divide power equally among themselves, ushering in a period of *Democracy*. This period of democratic rule is short-lived, however, and is replaced by *Tyranny*, upon the emergence of a 'popular leader who knows how to exploit the class antagonism between the rich and the poor within the democratic state, and who succeeds in building up a bodyguard or a private army of his own. The people who have hailed him first as a champion of freedom are soon enslaved; and then they must fight for him in "one war after another which he must stir up . . . because he must make the people feel the need of a general"' (Popper, 1945/2006a; 44). Each new stage in this historical journey of the state from its most just manifestation to its most abject is brought about by destabilising tendencies, motives, and emotions among its members. Greed, vested interest, emotion, passion: these things throw the state off balance and, hence, need to be guarded against if justice is to reign. Consequently, Plato argued, the state should be purged of those things which inflame these subversive passions and tendencies and, hence, the role of the political rulers is, as far as possible, to banish from society the possibility of change and disunity by quelling internal dissent, establishing a strict division of labour, and centralising power among a ruling elite who had undergone a rigid programme of indoctrination and training so that they might rule effectively (and without concern for personal advancement or ambition).

Plato's claim that the just state should be protected against disharmony thus allowed him to justify enormous and egregious violations of individual freedoms in the aim of 'arresting change', Popper believed, and presented a picture of the just state as one which had a moral duty to intrude upon any and all aspects of human life in the interests of rooting out potential sources of disunity and instability. It also allowed him to justify the accumulation of all political power in the hands of those capable of seeing the realm of the Forms (and, consequently, the form of the state). For Plato did not believe that everyone was capable of knowing what the ideal state should look like, and specifically argued that only that elite class of philosophers capable of seeing and understanding the Form of the state should hold political power. Furthermore, the qualities necessary to understand the nature of the ideal state could be shaped by social and political life, but they could not be instilled in those who were not born with them. Consequently, the ability to rule was something that people were either born with or not: those born with the intelligence and insight to see the Form of the state should hold power; those who are not born with this insight should not.

For Popper, Plato's republic represents the apotheosis of the closed society, and a destruction of all those principles and ideals upon which a truly just (i.e. open) society should be based. It is characterized by a ruling elite – defined as a *race* – whose ability to wield political power is determined by birth. It embodies the widespread and profound suppression of *individual* free thought and opinion in the interests of maintaining the stability of the *group*, the destruction of any distinction between *public* and *private* through the politicization of all aspects of all lives within the republic, and a radical, politically-enforced *division of labour*: the state, Plato believed, runs best when its people are confined to roles that have ascribed to them by birth, are discouraged to think beyond the confines of these roles for any reason, and are denied the capacity to participate in the governance of their own republic or their own lives lest they cause disharmony, disunity, or change. People should do what they were born to do: those born with the skills to mend shoes should mend shoes, those born with the skills to build ships should build ships, and those born with the skills to rule should rule. Democracy is a corrupted and debased form of politics because, among other things, it places power in the hands of those who do not have the skills or the knowledge to be able to wield it appropriately (i.e. in pursuit of ends located in the realm of the Forms, which only certain people can see). In Plato, therefore, Popper identified that claim that, for the good of society as a whole, it is crucial that individuals do not seek to better themselves, or seek to stray beyond the confines of their ordained role in society, or to learn new things, in case they start to ask questions, to challenge authority, or do anything other than obey the master race of Guardians who watch over them.

In all this, Popper believes, Plato shows himself to be an enemy of freedom and the individual, and, hence, of an open society, founded upon liberal principles. He denies that all individuals, by virtue of their basic humanity, are in some sense equal, and equally capable of rational thought and action. He denies that people should be free to live their lives according to goals and values that they themselves have considered, and deemed worthwhile, rather than goals which have been forced upon them by birth (or, more accurately, by those powerful few who are able to define what skills people have and which they do not). He denies that there is any conceivable area of human life which should be considered beyond the reach of the state: our goals, our ideals, our very thoughts themselves must be controlled in the interests of the greater good. He denies that individuals might together converge on the appropriate response to moral or political questions through free discussion and democratic debate: instead, the answers to these kinds of questions are located in an idealized past, and are *revealed* or *discovered* by those who have the ability to do so, and then communicated to those too ignorant to know where to look. He denies that political leaders should draw their authority from the consent of the people, and hence, that the leaders must justify their actions in ways in which the people to whom they are accountable find agreeable and intelligible: instead, they draw their authority from an ideal vision of society to which only they are privy. And he denies the central liberal idea that as far as possible the state should support all individuals in their desire to live their own lives in their own way, and only act in those ways which are consistent with, and in defence of, the ability of all individuals to pursue their own freely chosen ends without coercion or constraint: instead, he believes that the state should at all times remain vigilant against individuals developing their own ideas, pursuing their own goals, questioning their rulers, or doing anything to upset the order and harmony imposed upon them from above.

Plato's conception of the ideal state is, on this view, nothing less than totalitarianism – a state in which a minority assumes complete control of the majority, with the help of the military, and justifies the oppression and mistreatment of the people by appealing to a mythical future good for all human beings which only they can see, and which – therefore – only they can bring about. Understood thus, Plato's ideal republic does indeed share profound similarities with modern totalitarian states like Soviet communism under Stalin: the destruction of the family, the rejection of private property (for its tendency to cause conflicts), the suppression of art in the name of maintaining social harmony, the politicization of individuals' private lives in the interests of suppressing dissent, the denial of democracy or the idea of self-rule, the denial of individual freedom in the name of collective stability, and the constant, all pervasive, and dominating exercise of power among a chosen elite legitimated not by democratic or popular sovereignty, but by a utopian goal that only this elite could see or understand. To Popper, Plato's ideal republic represented little more or less than a system premised upon the domination of the racially inferior masses (who are denied education or the resources to challenge or to question the status quo) by the racially superior minority (who are indoctrinated, brain-washed, and purged of all individuality in order that they might rule without concern for personal status).

Popper was explicit in drawing the link between Plato's conception of justice and modern totalitarianism. He believed that the vision of the ideal state presented in Plato's work represented a direct philosophical pre-cursor to the modern totalitarianisms of Soviet communism, Italian fascism, and German Nazism. We can certainly see that it bore all the hallmarks of *historicism* (in terms of its politics and its sociology). Plato's sociology was *collectivist* and *holistic*, in that he believed that society should be understood not merely as a collection of individuals, but as an organic whole; his approach was *essentialist*, in the sense that he believed that it was crucial to grasp the fundamental essence of society before concluding as to how it should be structured; and his idea of justice was premised upon a conception of history as progressing according to discreet periods or epochs, brought about by identifiable social and political conditions.

These are claims that Plato shared with many historicist writers throughout history, but most obviously with the idealist writings of Hegel, and the materialist philosophy of Marx. However, while Popper felt that Plato's historicism was *pessimistic*, in that it presented historical development as a journey away from social harmony (and hence, justice) towards disharmony (and injustice), he described the historicism of Hegel and Marx as *optimistic*. Both Hegel and Marx believed that history progresses in a series of periods or *epochs* according to fixed laws of development, but – unlike Plato – believed that each stage in the development of society represents a *positive* step in the evolution of human social and political relations. Hegel, like Plato and Aristotle, adopted a methodologically *essentialist* approach to understanding society and the state: that is, like Plato and Aristotle, Hegel believed that it was crucial to grasp the fundamental essence of the state in order to work out how it had developed in the past, and how it might develop in the future. And like Aristotle, Hegel believed that natural phenomena developed towards a final cause or *telos*. The reason that Hegel was more optimistic about historical development than Plato, Popper argued, was because he understood the ideal form of the state to exist in the essence of each historical embodiment of the state in the world, rather than in some idealized past. For Hegel, therefore, the ongoing development of history served to further *reveal* the hidden or latent essence (and hence the ideal form of the state) in each successive historical period and therefore brought humanity closer to realizing it; it did not, as Plato believed, take humanity further *away* from it. Hegel's historicism is thus *optimistic* in the sense that the essences hidden within all phenomena (including the state) are 'self-moving; they are self-developing, or, using more fashionable terms, they are "emerging" and "self-creating". And they propel themselves in the direction of an Aristotelian "final cause", or, as Hegel puts it, towards a "self-realizing and self-realized cause in itself"' (Popper, 1945/2006b; 40). Hegel thus shared with Heraclitus and Plato the idea that the world was in a state of flux, but unlike them concluded that this was a good thing; Hegel's world of flux represented a 'state of "emergent" or "creative evolution"; each of its stages contains the preceding ones, from which it originates; and each stage supersedes all previous stages, approaching nearer and nearer to perfection. The general law of development is thus one of progress' (Popper, 1945/2006b; 40); the process by which the essences of all things are systematically revealed through the dialectical clash of ideas.

Despite the optimistic strain of Hegelian historicism, Popper argued that Hegel's philosophy was little more than 'the fertilizer to which modern totalitarianism owes its rapid growth' (Popper, 1945/2006b; 63). The reason for this, he thinks, is that we find in Hegel all the arguments and philosophical suppositions which would later be used by totalitarian dictators around the world to centralize power in the hands of an all-powerful state. Behind what Popper clearly viewed as purposefully obtuse and jargon-ridden prose, Hegel's theory of history was little more than a story about the rise of nationalism, and the journey of the State towards totalitarianism. Like Plato, he argued, Hegel envisages the state as an organism and, 'following Rousseau, who had furnished it with a "general will" Hegel furnishes it with a conscious, thinking essence, its "reason" or "Spirit". This Spirit . . . is at the very same time the collective *Spirit of the Nation* that forms the state' (Popper, 1945/2006b; 41). Thus to understand the State, we must understand its essence or Spirit, and to do *that* we must understand its history. 'The Spirit of the nation determines its historical destiny; and every nation that wishes "to emerge into existence" must assert its individuality or soul by entering the "Stage of History", that is to say, by fighting the other nations; the object of the fight is world domination' (Popper, 1945/2006b; 41).

Popper therefore identified in Hegel the idea that history develops according to overarching laws of development, and that the prime mover of history – its 'chosen people' – is the *nation.* History is the movement of the nation from a brutish, lawless rabble to a galvanized, militarized unity under the state. History is thus the march towards the nation-state: the all-powerful state being the Idea which is slowly but surely revealed within the essence of each successive historical epoch by dialectical leaps of will and imagination, until it is revealed entirely and the development of history ceases. Thus, in Hegel, we see the claim that 'the Nation State is . . . the absolute power on earth', and, as in Plato, we can see the exultation of the closed society over the open society.

Given its core assumptions, Popper believed, it was relatively easy for disciples of Hegel like Haekel to use Hegelianism to justify a particularly odious form of nationalism based on race. And in Hegel's exaltation of the nation state as the purest expression of freedom, and his claim that '"the State is . . . the basis and centre of all the concrete elements in the life of a people: of Art, Law, Morals, Religion, and Science"' Popper saw the defence of the totalitarian state whose 'might must permeate and control the whole life of the people in all its functions' (Hegel quoted in Popper, 1945/2006b; 68). Hegel's philosophy thus embodies all the worst excesses of historicism in its essentialism, holism, collectivism, and its subordination of the freedom and the interests of the individual to the good of the whole, and to the inexorable march of history. In his valuing of human passion and will, and of blood and war, Hegel – for Popper – did more than anyone to let loose on the world the destructive energies of nationalism and tribalism, and can be held responsible for furnishing tyrants and dictators ever since with the philosophical resources they needed to justify their corrupt and bankrupt appeal to tribal politics and to shun the open society character- ized by freedom, equality, reason, and individuality.

We find similar criticisms in Popper's treatment of Marx. While Popper had vastly higher regard for Marx than Hegel (or, it seems, for Plato), he nevertheless believed Marx to be a more radical historicist than either of them. For while Plato and Hegel were committed to a conception of politics driven by, and shaped according to, historical laws of development, they nevertheless believed that the historical process could be changed or guided by human intervention. Having identified what caused the state to develop towards injustice, for example, Plato outlined all the various ways in which it was possible for human actors to *stop* this process. Similarly, Hegel's dialectics were driven by *people* – their ideas, their passions, the conflicts between them – and, hence, for him history was a story of the development of human ideas and the national traditions which shaped them. For Marx, however, there was very little room for human beings to affect the development of history at all. Marx's inversion of Hegel's idealism took the laws of historical deve- lopment out of the hands of human beings entirely and located them instead in wider, impersonal economic forces. He subscribed to a social and historical *determinism*:

> if there was to be a social science, and accordingly, historical prophecy, the main course of history must be pre-determined, and neither good-will nor reason had the power to alter it. All that was left to us in the way of reasonable interference was to make sure, by historical prophecy, of the impending course of development, and to remove the obstacles in its path. (Popper, 1945/2006b; 94)

As Marx himself put it in *Das Kapital*, when 'society has discov- ered the natural law that determines its own movement, . . . even then it can neither overleap the natural phases of its evolution, nor shuffle them out of the world by a stroke of the pen. But this much it can do; it can shorten and lessen its birth-pangs' (quoted in Popper, 1945/2006b; 94).

Consequently, the roles of the social scientist and of the social engineer for Marx were clear. The social scientist should seek to determine the precise social and economic conditions under which capitalism would collapse and be replaced by communism, and the social engineer should seek to reform society in such a way as to hasten this collapse. This, as we have indicated, requires the social engineer and the social scientist to take a *collectivist* and *holistic* approach to understanding society: an approach which takes as its principal aim the piecing together of the ways in which societies (and political institutions) evolve in response to developments in the economic 'base'. Marx himself provided a detailed sketch of this process, most famously in his *Preface to A Contribution to the Critique of Political Economy*. While liberals and others believed that individual consciousness shaped and determined the character of social, political and economic arrangements, Marx famously believed the opposite: that the social, political, and (most importantly) economic conditions under which one lived shaped and determined one's consciousness (by which he meant one's ideas, preferences, and values, one's understanding of the world, and of one's place within it). Human consciousness was thus, for Marx, intimately tied to the particular social and historical environment in which we find ourselves, and was determined by it. This is why we come to accept capitalism, even though it has devastating consequences for our lives and our humanity. We draw our understanding of the world, our ideas, our ambitions and commitments from the network of social relations in which we are located, and these are in turn determined by economic forces. Hence, the capitalist system itself determines what we know and what we do not know about the world, and thus stifles criticism: capitalism robs us of our humanity, alienates us from those things which make us human, commodifies our productive labour power, and encourages us to think of ourselves as isolated individuals in relations of competition with one another, each with our own interests and preferences and 'rights', rather than cooperative members of a shared community, and in doing all these things, capitalism renders it impossible for us to gain the requisite critical distance from our circumstances to reflect upon them meaningfully or to criticize them. The role of the Marxist social engineer, then, is to help encourage those circumstances in which human beings might come to realize the many and varied ways in which the capitalist system brutalizes them and undermines their humanity. The continued development of capitalism will (to put it in Hegelian terms) reveal the inconsistencies within the essence, and its flaws will become more obvious to the people who live within it. When these inconsistencies become so obvious as to be untenable, and so clearly unjust as to be unconscionable, human beings will rise up and seek to change the system, thus ushering in a new historical period of communism. For Marx, then, there is a role for political and social action, but it is a very restricted one, limited merely to the establishment of conditions under which the working class might fully grasp the extent of their oppression, and seek to do something about it.

For Popper, then, Marx's claim that it 'is not the consciousness of man that determines his existence – rather, it is his social existence that determines his consciousness' represents an important critique of psychologism (which Popper praised) but also underwrites a 'conspiracy theory of society' (Popper, 1963/2007b; eg. 165), and the impotence of human beings (and politics) in the face of overwhelming historical forces beyond their control. It wrongly encourages us to think that our opinions and ideas are not really ours, and that not only our actions but our *thoughts* are determined by others, or by history itself. This is why Popper felt that Marxism was the 'purest' form of historicism: not only does it negate the capacity of individuals to act freely, or to change the social and political world in which they live according to their own ideas about the world, it suggests that the deepest and most personal ideas that people might have (e.g. their sense of self, their loves, fears, hopes, ambitions) are determined by *history*, and by the historical laws of development in particular. It is not possible for individual people to exert their will on society such that they can bring about change, because the content of their will is determined by the very social, political, and economic relations that they would seek to change. All they can do is wait until the economic conditions in which they find themselves develop to such an extent that the internal inconsistencies inherent within the capitalist system are revealed; only then, when the time is right, can human beings rise up and usher in the new social and political system, as demanded by the new prevailing economic conditions. What the 'conspiracy theory of society' suggests, then, is that people cannot form their own authentic opinions and are at the mercy of the designs of powerful individuals and groups. Popper felt that this view rendered individuals invisible in the historical process, and, worse, allowed Marx to deny or ignore their expressed preferences. Anyone who disagreed with Marx's philosophical vision could be easily denounced as suffering from 'false consciousness'; indeed the fact that they disagreed with Marx was seen as proving Marx's point, rather than undermining it, and was merely seen as testament to the power of the capitalist system to dupe the people into thinking that all was well when it really was not. Having argued as much, it thus became relatively straightforward to justify political action on the basis that it is what the people *would* want if only they could free themselves from the imprisoning ideology of capitalism, rather than what they actually *say* they want.

Popper felt that he had identified innumerable problems in Marx's philosophy, and it is simply impossible to go into all of them here. Suffice to say that he believed that Marx, more than any other, introduced the evils of historicism to the study of the social sciences and politics, and as such represents a considerable threat to those disciplines, and to the quest for the open society. Popper found Marx's philosophy unpersuasive because it embodies in their most pure forms the central historicist claims that (a) it is possible and appropriate to prophesize the future development of society by revealing overarching laws of historical development, (b) in order to understand *individuals* we must first understand the social *wholes* (classes, societies, nations, cultures, etc.) in which they exist, and hence, that social science should be *methodologically collectivist*, (c) in order to understand societies (and the individuals within them) we need to grasp the fundamental *nature* or *structure* of the social whole (i.e. as determined by economic forces which are always developing), and hence, that we need to adopt an approach which is *methodologically essentialist*, (d) it is possible, and appropriate, to justify social and political reforms on the basis of whether or not they help to bring about the predestined fate of humankind (for which people may or may not express support), and (e) that individual human beings are powerless before the overarching and impersonal laws of development, which constrain them, stifle their ability to form their own judgments about the world in which they live, and determine their every thought and action.

The Open Society

Popper believed that historicist social and political thought produced a theory of the state that was thoroughly obnoxious, corrupt, and oppressive, and represented a vindication of the closed society. He also thought it was rooted in an utterly flawed methodology and a mistaken epistemology. He therefore believed that we need to reject the normative and epistemological ideas at the heart of historicism and replace them with a form of politics which is premised upon, and compatible with, his wider ideas about epistemology. As soon as we acknowledge that no group or individual (whether they be a scientist or a social scientist or a political leader) can claim to know the *truth*, we must acknowledge that no individual, institution, or social practice can be considered *infallible* or *unquestionable*. In the absence of infallible truth, it is left for individuals to work out among themselves what the role of political institutions should be, what public policies should be implemented, and what are the ends of politics. Just as science should not be understood as the pursuit of great *truths* or *proofs* but rather the resolution of problems through the elimination of *errors* in those theories which currently exist, so politics should not be understood as the pursuit of great *truths* or *ideals*, but rather the elimination of those social *problems* which afflict society, through the elimination of *errors* made by, or embodied in, social and political institutions. Popper therefore subscribed to what he called a 'negative utilitarianism': the point of social science and politics is not to encourage general pleasure or welfare, but to minimize harm and suffering by identifying the sources of such harm, and reforming them in a piecemeal way. This held for the design of social and political *institutions*, and public *policies*.

According to Popper's commitment to negative utilitarianism, and his rejection of utopianism, social and political *institutions* should not be designed so as to provide individual rulers or elites with the ability to pursue some ideal good, but rather to prevent them from 'doing too much damage' (Popper, 1945/ 2006b; 142). That is, the legal framework of an open society is one conceived as a set of 'protective institutions' rather than a set of rules which enable rulers to exercise their will at any given time. State intervention in the social and economic life of individuals will sometimes be necessary, then, but these interventions can only be justified if they are the carried out by institutions which have been designed to protect individuals (and their freedom) and which have themselves grown in a piecemeal fashion as a consequence of accumulated knowledge, experience, and critique. They cannot be justified if they are the mere products of some ruler's will. The principle of institutional design underwritten by Popper's negative utilitarianism and his critical rationalism is thus one which enshrines piecemeal social engineering, and the rejection of radical change, at its heart. Reform can be concrete and enduring, but reforms must be rooted in an appreciation of what has worked in the past and what has not, and what led us to where we currently are. And the way in which we achieve our long-term ends (and these ends themselves) must be subject to critique and possible rejection in the light of all the contrary arguments that the world can provide. The point of institutions, then, is to provide a necessary check on the power of leaders and to quell the possibility of radical (and thus, irresponsible) change, by supporting important individual freedoms and an environment in which persons might engage with one another in democratic dialogue. In addition to protecting the freedom of individual citizens, and society from irresponsible changes, Popper believed that his approach had a further benefit: that the legal framework 'can be known and understood by the individual citizen'. Indeed, he felt, the system 'should be designed to be so understandable. Its functioning is predictable. It introduces a factor of certainty and security into social life . . . As opposed to this, the method of personal intervention must introduce an ever-growing element of unpredictability into social life, and it will develop the feeling that social life is irrational and insecure' (Popper, 1945/2006b; 143).

With regard to *policies*, Popper's negative utilitarianism embodied a rejection of any justification which appealed to some long-term future good, and emphasized instead the piecemeal identification and resolution of concrete social problems. The most obvious social evils that have thus far been identified and which 'can be remedied, or relieved, by social cooperation' include, he believed, 'poverty, unemployment and similar forms of social insecurity, sickness and pain, penal cruelty, slavery and other forms of serfdom, religious and racial forms of discrimination, lack of educational opportunities, rigid class differences, and war' (Popper, 1963/2007b; 497–8). It is the responsibility of the institutions of the open society to tackle these problems in a spirit of critical rationalism, and in a way which is consistent with Popper's wider claims about epistemology, the growth of knowledge, anti-radicalism, and the importance of experience.

Consequently, neither policies nor institutions should be measured according to criteria which only a chosen few can see, but according to much more procedural, short-term criteria, like whether the particular institutions or policies do the job that they are supposed to do, or whether the social problems that are currently being addressed are the right ones, and being addressed in the most efficient way. The point of politics, Popper believed, was not to draw up unsustainable blueprints, or dream of ideal societies, but to identify those social, political, and economic problems currently facing society, and to seek efficient, justifiable, and progressive solutions to these problems. Once again, social engineering should be *piecemeal* rather than utopian, and based upon a public debate about political priorities, the ends to which institutions should be aimed, and whether those institutions themselves could be reformed or replaced. Unlike utopian social engineers, who would have us believe that the only valuable form of social experiments are large-scale ones, piecemeal social engineers acknowledge the value in small-scale, short-term experiments and proposals: the

> introduction of a new kind of life insurance, of a new kind of taxation, of a new penal reform, are all social experiments which have their repercussions through the whole of society without remodelling society as a whole . . . the kind of experiment from which we can learn most is the alteration of one social institution at a time. For only in this way can we learn how to fit institutions into the framework of other institutions, and how to adjust them so that they can work according to our intentions. And only in this way can we make mistakes, and learn from our mistakes, without rising repercussions of a gravity that must endanger the will to future reforms. (Popper, 1945/2006a; 172)

Utopianism is contrary to the scientific method and the growth of knowledge (and hence, to the identification and resolution of social and political problems) because, like the inductive model of science on which it is based, it encourages us to cling to theories in the face of evidence of their failure, rather than to embrace their failure, to learn from our mistakes, and propose new – and falsifiable – theories in their place.

Popper's conception of politics was therefore one which took individual freedom very seriously, and sought to defend individuals from arbitrary interference and oppression. Above all, it sought to free individuals from the tyranny of established and unquestionable truths, and was committed to providing all persons with the political, economic, and intellectual resources necessary to protect them against what Mill (following Tocqueville) called the tyranny of the majority. Individual freedom could not be subordinated to the good of the social whole, or sacrificed in the interests of achieving social unity, stability, or national unity. The organic collectivism and essentialism at the heart of historicism should be abandoned and replaced with methodological individualism and nominalism. No longer should individuals feel that their interests and ideals and ambitions are unimportant in the face of the overarching needs of society or the vast and impenetrable forces of history. And no longer should social and political scientists seek to grasp the fundamental *essence* of states and societies in order to work out how they should be structured and what policies should be implemented. Individuals should be afforded the resources they need to throw off the shackles of tribalism and nationalism (the 'politics of the group') and which encourage people to think of themselves as little more or less than members of some wider, and mythologized, social whole possessing a destiny of its own which trumps theirs. Individuals should be given the resources they need to develop their capacity to engage with others in debates about politics; they should be able to work out their own views about the rightful ends of social and political institutions, they should be able to express these views, and they should be able to act upon them in ways which feed into the democratic system. The authority of particular institutions or individuals is never fixed, just as the arguments and philosophical positions which provide their justification are never settled; rather, they are open to debate and question through an ongoing process of democratic dialogue conducted – as it is in science or in any other field – between equals who have adopted a critical rationalist approach to existing social and political theories, proposals, social practices, and institutions. Just as public debate about existing theories in the physical sciences establishes a form of *objectivity* among those involved, so the public debate of social scientific and political questions establishes a similar kind of objectivity or impartiality: public debates about politics weed out arguments based on duplicity, deceit or manipulation, and force those in charge to justify their actions to the people in ways that they can comprehend and find acceptable.

Popper's political vision was thus one rooted in the importance of individual freedom, democracy, and the idea that social problems could be identified, tentatively understood, and resolved through a process of debate framed in terms of a trial and error process of conjecture and refutation, in which no-one could claim to know the ultimate and final truth, and in which all current theories were falsifiable, and hence up for debate. In the absence of infallible truth, there can be no ultimate good for all individuals which can be assumed to afford legitimacy to particular institutions, practices, or people, or which set forever the problems to which institutions should attend: all we can do is approach each and every political question as rigorously and innovatively as possible, which means testing our existing social and political theories against the sum total of all that we know about the world in the interests of falsifying them.

In place of nationalism, Popper defended an optimistic internationalism – a cosmopolitan politics rooted in the uniting vision of humanity as rational and free. Plato believed that 'opinion is shared by all men; but reason is shared only by Gods, and by very few men' (Popper, 1945/2006a; 252). Hegel subordinated the importance of reason to passion and will, and hence, sought a politics of national belonging. Popper was a fallibilist about reason, and counselled against the naïve view that reasoned reflection could provide certain knowledge, and rejected what he saw as a blind faith among some Enlightenment thinkers in the ability of reason to provide social and political blueprints. However, he nevertheless united with liberals and rationalists throughout history in asserting the Enlightenment idea that the capacity for reason is possessed by all individuals, wherever they may live, and whatever groups they may belong to, and that it is this uniting capacity to reason which allows us to empathize with others, and to understand their pains: reason, 'supported by imagination, enables us to understand that men who are far away, whom we shall never see, are like ourselves . . . [B]y the use of thought and imagination, we may become ready to help all who need our help' (Popper, 1945/2006b; 265). No nation or state could appeal to history, or the good of the group, or traditional values, to dominate or oppress their people, and no political leader could claim refuge in the notion of national sovereignty in order to justify the violation of their peoples' individual freedoms.

Popper's commitment to freedom, reason, and critical rationalism were thus intimately linked, and held implications for domestic and international politics. Internationally, as we have said, it underwrote a liberal form of cosmopolitanism, rooted in the moral equality of all human beings, and the need for international dialogue about how best to resolve social, political, and economic problems. Domestically, it mandated the reform of social and political institutions such that they were capable of protecting individual freedoms, and safeguarding the deliberative environment necessary for individual members of society to work out together – through reasoning with one another – how best to resolve social and political problems. Reason is not, as Plato believed, 'a kind of "faculty," which may be possessed and developed by different men in vastly different degrees. Admittedly, intellectual gifts may be different in this way, and they may contribute to reasonableness; but they need not. Clever men may be very unreasonable; they may cling to their prejudices and may not expect to hear anything worthwhile from others.' According to Popper, however,

> we not only owe our reason to others but we can never excel others in our reasonableness in a way that would establish a claim to authority; authoritarianism and rationalism in our sense cannot be reconciled, since argument, which includes criticism, and the art of listening to criticism, is the basis of reasonableness. Thus rationalism in our sense is diametrically opposed to all those modern Platonic dreams of brave new worlds in which the growth of reason would be controlled or 'planned' by some superior reason. Reason, like science, grows by way of mutual criticism; the only possible way of "planning" its growth is to develop those institutions that safeguard the freedom of this criticism, that is to say, the freedom of thought. (Popper, 1945/2006b; 253)

Thus, we find the claim (touched upon earlier) that human reason is embodied in, and can only flourish in the presence of, *institutions* which encourage and protect it: that reason is *public* in character.

Popper therefore believed in the possibility of progress, but of a very different kind to that defended by the historicists. His idea of *scientific* progress, for example, outlined in *The Poverty of Historicism*, held that the development of human knowledge was linked to, and dependent upon, particular institutions, namely, those institutions like speech and writing, as well institutions like laboratories, universities, and research facilities, in which scientists might engage in public debate about existing theories. Consequently, it was very important indeed that, in the interests of scientific progress, the right social institutions were present, by which he meant those institutions which protected and encouraged free debate. These claims connect sharply with Popper's wider claims about the role of institutions in driving *political* or *social* progress: if we value progress, the development of knowledge, freedom, and the capacity of social institutions to improve society by rectifying those problems which afflict society and undermine the basic equality of human beings – as we should – then we must establish and protect social institutions which allow us to debate with one another about the appropriate ends of politics, to form our own judgements about politics, and to criticize the judgments of others, while all the while defending our own views against the criticisms of others and, when necessary, rejecting our theories in favour of newer, more persuasive ones. Only the 'institutional method makes it possible to make adjustments in the light of discussion and experience', he argued.

> It alone makes it possible to apply the method of trial and error to our political actions. It is long-term; yet the permanent legal framework can be slowly changed, in order to make allowances for unforeseen and undesired consequences, for changes in other parts of the framework, etc. It alone allows us to find out, by experience and analysis, what we actually were doing when we intervened with a certain aim in mind. Discretionary decisions of the rulers or civil servants are outside these rational methods. They are short-term decisions, transitory, changing from day to day, or at best, from year to year. As a rule . . . they cannot even be publicly discussed, both because necessary information is lacking, and because the principles on which decision is taken are obscure. (Popper, 1945/2006b; 143)

Policies, if they do not do what they are supposed to do, should be dropped and replaced with ones which do. Institutions, if they prove themselves unfit to carry out the tasks required of them, should be reformed so as to be better able to meet the social and political challenges at hand. And politicians, if they prove themselves incapable of ruling effectively, should be removed in favour of ones who are better suited to public office. All of these decisions – including the prior questions concerning the appropriate role of institutions and policies and politicians – are, in an open society, decided by free and equal citizens, engaged in reasonable democratic debate with one another via institutions which protect their individual freedoms. Thus, while historicists defended essentialism, holism, utopian social engineering, totalitarianism, and the subordination of the individual to society and to impersonal laws of historical development, Popper defended nominalism, individualism, piecemeal social engineering, democracy, and the importance of each and every individual in their own right, not as mere tools to be used and manipulated in the interests of bringing about some ideal state of affairs, but as ends in themselves.

3

Reception and Influence of Popper's Philosophy

Many of Popper's interventions in epistemology, scientific method, and political philosophy were, in their time, ground-breaking, original, and radical. His influence in these areas is significant: it is not possible to study the philosophy of the natural sciences without engaging with Popper's work, and it is arguably impossible to grasp the significance of a lot of the work in this area without being familiar with what Popper had to say. In tackling some of the most fundamental questions in epistemology and science in the way that it did, Popper's work was inspirational, and influenced some of the most notable philosophers of science in the history of the discipline. Major contributions to the philosophy of science by Joseph Agassi (Popper's student and research assistant at the LSE) and John Watkins, for example, draw explicitly upon Popper's ideas in order to defend the possibility of scientific discovery in the face of scepticism (Agassi, 1993; Watkins, 1984). Imre Lakatos sought to bridge Popper's evolutionary epistemology with Thomas Kuhn's conception of science as a revolutionary endeavour (Lakatos, 1976, 1978a, and 1978b). And for a generation of philosophers of science, Popper's work has provided the backdrop against which contemporary debates about induction, deduction, truth, and knowledge are conducted. This is not to say that they all agree with him, of course. Paul Feyerabend, for example, initially impressed with Popper's approach, later rejected Popper's theory of falsificationism as too restrictive, and argued instead for a form of scientific anarchism in place of overarching, all-encompassing methodologies (Feyerabend, 1975/1993). Several thinkers, including Hilary Putnam, criticized Popper's description of falsification on the grounds that it was insufficiently attentive to the extent to which any theory could be 'immunized' against refutation; this criticism led Popper to move the idea of verisimilitude – the idea that existing theories should be replaced with ones which better approximate the truth – more centrally in his theory (Putnam, 1974). W. V. O. Quine and Pierre Duhem, both proposed that the falsification of theories was complicated by the fact that it was impossible to test individual hypotheses in isolation, as each theory was inextricably part of a wider network of theories, each of which were mutually dependent upon one another (Duhem, 1954; Quine, 1960). And Thomas Kuhn's *The Structure of Scientific Revolutions* published in 1962 provided an alternative account of scientific discovery as a process of revolutionary developments (or 'paradigm shifts') which, he thought, better described the way in which scientists actually worked. Popper's response to Kuhn's influential book was to suggest (in 'The Myth of the Framework') that Kuhn's claims about the incommensurability of scientific paradigms were rooted in the same fallacious assumptions which stifled the growth of knowledge and justified moral and social relativism (Popper, 1994a).

Poverty and, in particular, *The Open Society* also drew praise from a broad and diverse group of thinkers from across the political spectrum. For example, socialists like Bertrand Russell and Harold Laski were keen to defend *The Open Society* for its critique of *laissez-faire* economics and its vindication of a non-Marxist form of social democracy. Meanwhile, philosophers and economists from the political Right like Hayek, von Mises, and Milton Friedman admired Popper's work and used it to bolster their critique of social and economic planning, and their vindication of free markets and political gradualism. His work on the social sciences represented an important contribution to debates among economists like Carl Menger (1871/1981), Ludwig von

Mises (1949), and Karl Polanyi (1944/2001) about the role of history, essentialism, and the state in the study of economics, but did not do so from within any specific ideological position.

Popper's influence on the development of liberal, conservative, libertarian, socialist, and social democratic thought in the twentieth century can – and has been – drawn by many philosophers and historians (e.g. Magee, 1973; Miller, 1994; Shearmur, 1996). The fact that his political thought has been adopted and defended by so many very different thinkers is a testament to its ingenuity and enduring appeal, but also presents a conundrum which goes beyond Popper and into the methodology of political thought more generally. Was Popper a conservative? Was he a libertarian? Was he a social democrat? Such questions are complicated by the indeterminacy of *isms* in general, and of conservatism and libertarianism in particular, as we will see in the next section. But they are also complicated by Popper's unwillingness to define many of his foundational commitments, and the tensions inherent in his dual role as scholar and polemicist. Popper's language and tone in *The Open Society* angered many enemies and led many potential allies to dismiss his work as unscholarly. Popper was certainly not one to suffer fools gladly. In *The Open Society*, we must recall, Popper accuses Plato (probably the most respected and venerated figure in the history of Western civilization) of, among other things, hating freedom, deliberately misrepresenting the philosophy of Socrates for his own selfish ends, advocating the deliberate slaughter of racially inferior members of society, and coming up with the rule of the 'philosopher king' in order to provide a justification for why Plato himself should hold power. He calls Marx a 'false prophet', Fichte a 'fraud' and a 'windbag', and describes Aristotle (probably the second most respected and venerated figure in the history of Western civilization) as 'not a man of striking originality of thought' (although he did 'invent logic', for which Popper believed he should be thanked). He variously described the philosophy of Hegel as 'bombastic and hysterical', 'indigestible', and 'outstanding in its lack of originality'. Indeed, 'as far as

Hegel is concerned,' he claimed, 'I do not even think he was talented . . . There is nothing in Hegel's writing that has not been said better before him' (Popper, 1945/2006b; 35). Furthermore, in a number of places, Popper cites approvingly Schopenhauer's description of Hegel as a 'flat-headed, insipid, nauseating, illiterate charlatan, who reached the pinnacle of audacity in scribbling together and dishing up the craziest mystifying nonsense' (quoted in Popper, 1945/2006b; 36). Clearly, to Popper, Hegel was little more than a 'clown': a hopeless apologist for Frederick William of Prussia, who adopted a deliberately baffling written style in order that he might confuse his readers into thinking that originality lay where it did not.

It is therefore hardly surprising that following the publication of *The Open Society* in 1945, many leapt to defend Plato, Aristotle, Marx and Hegel, claiming that Popper had made huge and grievous errors in his interpretation of their works and its implications. Plato scholars, in particular, were aggrieved. Despite the emergence of a number of works criticizing Plato for his antipathy towards democracy (e.g. Fite, 1934; Crossman, 1959; and Winspear, 1940), there existed a broad consensus among classical scholars and historians that Plato represented a voice for humanity and reason. Popper's vicious attack was genuinely shocking, not merely in respect of what he said, but the way in which he said it. Most classicists responded with polemical reviews, and two – John Wild and Ronald Levinson – even wrote monograph length defences of Plato against Popper's critique (Levinson, 1953; Wild, 1953). The problem, it seemed, was not only that Popper had misread Plato and Aristotle, but that he had accorded them insufficient respect. John Plamenatz, for example, described Popper's treatment of Aristotle as exhibiting the manner that 'an unkind man sometimes adopts towards someone whom he believes to be his intellectual inferior; and, as is usual in such cases, it tells us more about the contemnor than the object of his contempt' (Plamenatz, 1952/1967; 267). The dominant feeling among classicists was (and still is) that Popper's strident, often polemical, prose missed many nuances and intricacies in Plato's thought which would have complicated Popper's interpretation. They pointed out, for example, that a closer, more sympathetic reading of *The Republic* showed that Plato's eugenics was not straightforwardly 'fascist' in the way that Popper maintained, that classical Athens was not as obviously progressive or open as Popper suggested, and that Popper's idealization of Athenian imperialism was unrealistic and based on inaccuracy. There is also little evidence to support Popper's claim that Socrates was committed to critical rationalism, individualism, and equalitarianism, as Popper defined them, and many rejected the claim that Plato was a historicist in the sense that Popper implied, arguing that Plato's theory of the Forms appealed to philosophical ideals rather than historical ones.

Popper's critique of Marx has been similarly criticized for being too narrow and simplistic. For example, he discussed neither Marx's *Economic and Philosophical Manuscripts of 1844,* which came out in German in 1932, and which many take to be one of Marx's most important works, nor the *Grundrisse,* which did not appear in German until 1939. Furthermore, Popper failed to engage with the work of other important Marxists such as Gramsci and Sorel (who rejected the notion of inevitable change), and although in 'the early 1920s, Lukacs frequented the barracks where Popper was living . . . Popper seemed unfamiliar with *History and Class Consciousness* (1923) and the controversy surrounding it. He knew of Rosa Luxemburg and witnessed the council movement in Vienna, but there was no mention of them in *The Open Society.* He ignored the Austro-Marxists: Adler, most of Bauer, Hilferding, and Renner. One could hear echoes of Bauer's political essays, but that was all' (Hacohen, 2000; 440–1). Despite his professed respect for Marx, Popper seemed unwilling to extend him the courtesy of debating his ideas in all their complexity, or in dealing with the various ways in which his ideas had been interpreted, refined, and restated by his followers. Rather than present Marxism as a dynamic, evolving creed which animated many intelligent and committed people, and which was the subject of great debate inside and outside the academy, Popper attacked Marx as a false prophet of historicism, and seemed uninterested in wider debates or applications of his conclusions. His critique of Marx thus seemed rather abstract and austere, cut off from the rich tradition of thought in which Marx's work was embedded.

Many critics also took issue with the substance of Popper's critique. They argued, for example, that Popper falsely attributed to Marx a view that politics was impotent in the face of economic change (e.g. Cornforth, 1968). They also suggested that, among other things, he misunderstood the relationship between Marx and Hegel and underestimated the importance of individuals and classes in the collapse of capitalism. However, Popper at least tried to provide a coherent critique of Marx which was balanced with a broad appreciation of Marx's intentions and motivations: to alleviate poverty, and to understand the character of capitalist economics and society such that its principal evils might be transcended. Popper's furious denunciation of Hegel (to which he devoted a mere 80 pages out of *The Open Society's* 900), on the other hand, seems to be as driven by indignation as analytical rigour. It is by no means as thorough as his treatment of Plato and Marx, despite his claims that Hegel represents the 'source of all modern historicism' (Popper, 1945/2006b; 30), and hence, the source of the principal threat facing the practice and study of politics in the modern era. Hegel scholars then and since have had little time for Popper's views, and have not taken them seriously. Critics were quick to point out that instead of engaging directly with Hegel's writings, Popper had appeared to rely almost entirely on a single edited anthology – *Hegel Selections* edited by J. Loewenberg – as his source: a book which was intended for students and contained not a single complete work. Similarly, in order to establish Hegel's link with the Nazis, Popper drew heavily on the work of Aurel Kolnai, quoting substantially from his book *The War Against the West*. But many of Kolnai's claims were (and remain) very controversial. Popper, however, simply stated them as the truth, often quoting them out of context. There appears to be little or no evidence that Popper checked the reliability of these claims for himself, or drew his own independent conclusions as to their viability (see Popper, 1945/2006b; 354). Furthermore, critics suggested that in the interests of establishing a more or less clear development from Hegel to Nazism, Popper seemed to confuse and simplify the intellectual relationship between diverse thinkers like Husserl, Scheler, Heidegger and Jaspers – exaggerating the links between them, ameliorating differences, and spuriously drawing together disparate themes and ideas. Moreover, he repeatedly defended the work of thinkers like Schopenhauer and J. F. Fries against the proto-Nazi Hegel, seemingly unaware that both Fries and Schopenhauer had at one time or another expressed anti-Semitic views (Kauffman, 1959). Defenders of Hegelianism like Walter Kauffman and Charles Taylor united with many others in suggesting that Popper had profoundly misunderstood Hegel's metaphysics, and misinterpreted Hegel's defence of the state as justifying a policy of racial purity (Taylor, 1958).

More broadly, Popper was accused of leaving his central target – totalitarianism – underdetermined and undefined. Just as it appeared he had little interest in engaging with the wider literature on Hegel, Plato, or Marx, Popper also appeared to have little interest in discussing wider work on totalitarianism, or in defining totalitarianism in anything more than the broadest possible terms. This is important because Popper's understanding of totalitarianism differed radically from that of many modern writers. Most theories of totalitarianism existing at that time emphasized its uniquely modern character, in particular its links with modern industry and technology (e.g. Arendt, 1951/2004; Brzezinski, 1956). Popper, on the other hand, suggested that totalitarianism had existed in one form or another in the writings of thinkers as historically distant as Plato and Heraclitus. In making these claims, Popper seemed to feel it unnecessary to engage with the steadily growing literature on the nature, origins, and character of the totalitarian state (e.g. Aron, 1957). Instead, Popper left his conception of totalitarianism – and, hence, the central enemy of the open society – vague.

Similarly, although in *Poverty* Popper spends a great deal of time reconstructing historicist arguments in the most favourable light (in the interests of 'building up a position really worth attacking' (Popper, 1957/2005; 3)) it is striking that virtually all the references intended to corroborate his assertions about 'what historicists think' are to one book: Karl Mannheim's *Man and Society*. Popper clearly thought that Mannheim's approach to social and political science was mistaken, however it is not clear how accurate or fair Popper's interpretation of Mannheim is, or how easily Mannheim's views can be seen as a template for other historicists throughout history, from Plato and Heraclitus to Hegel, Marx, Mill and Comte. Once again, critics have suggested, we see in *Poverty* (as in *The Open Society*) an unwillingness by Popper to engage with specific arguments by specific thinkers, and a tendency to lump many different thinkers together in order to damn them all at once.

Defenders of Popper like Bryan Magee have sought to counter the common charge of unscholarly methods by emphasizing the intentions behind *Poverty* and *The Open Society* and the context in which they were written. Popper, we must recall, described *The Open Society* as a 'fighting book'. He wrote it quickly whilst in exile in New Zealand, having left a war torn Europe threatened by Fascism. If his tone is a little too strident in places, or if his treatment of certain venerated historical thinkers is unfair or partial, supporters say, it is because Popper was driven by a moral determination to rid the world of the ideas which gave birth to the evils which threatened the world at that time. Popper wrote *The Open Society* in New Zealand amid fears that the Japanese would reach them in a matter of months. Europe was under threat from domination by the Nazis. There was simply no time to read the complete works of Hegel and Marx, or to engage in extended debate about the philosophical, historical, or linguistic complexities introduced by contemporary scholars of Plato, or contemporary Marxists or Hegelians: the world needed a defence of the open society and quick. One might well concede that such an endeavour had a place. However, it does not sit easily with Popper's wider views about the growth of knowledge and the proper conduct of academic debate. Magee has suggested that Popper was not interested in cheap-shots, and that his approach was always to construct the strongest and most positive account of his opponents' theories before demolishing their core points (Magee, 1973). On such a view, Popper thus could be said to practice what he preached by adopting the norms of critical rationalism in his own work. He certainly claimed that this was his intention in *Poverty* and his work in the philosophy of the natural sciences. Profound disagreement continues to exist, however, as to whether Popper used this approach in *The Open Society*. His treatment of Plato and Marx, though sometimes respectful, was vicious and unrelenting, and – many felt – based upon a partial and deliberately sketchy appreciation of the literature in the field. Even fewer disagree about whether he tried to show Hegel in his best light before attempting to demolish his entire philosophy: he quite clearly had no interest in doing so, and had no good word to say about him or his philosophy. Describing his treatment of Hegel some years later, Popper said that 'I neither could nor wished to spend unlimited time upon deep researches into the history of a philosopher whose work I abhor' (Popper, 1945/2006b; 446). Whatever one may say about Hegel, this statement clearly violates Popper's own claims about the necessary conduct of intellectual debate, and raises the interesting question as to whether or not Popper's ideas concerning Hegel (and perhaps, Marx and Plato) can, on Popper's own terms, represent a meaningful contribution to knowledge.

Popper, Burke, and the fallibility of reason

Nevertheless, Popper's work in social and political thought has proved influential to thinkers across the political spectrum. Popper's steadfast unwillingness to be labelled as the exponent of any particular ideology meant that supporters and critics alike could draw on his work to defend or criticize a wide variety of philosophical and political positions, including libertarianism, classical liberalism, social democracy, and socialism. Popper would have recoiled at the idea that he was espousing an ideology, although he would have had some sympathy for the idea of a tradition (understood appropriately). It is precisely this anti-ideologism in Popper's thought which, for many, brings him within the conservative tradition. Conservatism, in its various historical guises, has often been at least partly characterized by its rejection of ideology. Its defenders have often seen it as more as an *approach* to understanding society and political authority, rather than a set of principles with normative content. Conservatives have, on the whole, defined themselves as pragmatists, more interested in identifying and responding to social problems by appealing to the accumulated wisdom contained within existing traditions, institutions, and values, than in appealing to principles which define some specified and ideal future.

Put this way, we can already see some of the ways in which we might want to call Popper a conservative. However, conservatism has changed in the course of its history, and it is important to understand these changes if we are to grasp Popper's association with it. Until the late 1970s and early 1980s, Conservatism had been traditionally associated with the works of thinkers like Edmund Burke. It was primarily a theory about authority and political reform. Burke famously denounced the French revolution, and the Enlightenment principles upon which it was based, as a travesty, claiming that the Enlightenment represented merely a collection of vague mistakes about human equality, reason, and the importance of freedom, and the revolution was nothing more than a violent attack on proper authority and tradition (Burke, 1790/1986). The events in France did not, he thought, mark the heralding of a new era of *liberte, egalite,* and *fraternite* as its defenders suggested; rather it represented a catastrophic break with those traditions in which the rightful authority of political leaders and institutions resided, and a casting aside of the accumulated knowledge and experience which might provide guidance as to how institutions should be structured, what their role might be, and who should most appropriately hold power. Burke defended political *gradualism* over political *radicalism*. The French revolution embodied the Enlightenment idea that it was possible to overthrow traditional hierarchies of power and privilege through the application of reason. Consequently, he believed, the revolutionaries were too optimistic about the power of reason to affect radical change. They were possessed of the impetuous and irresponsible notion that a just, functioning social and political order could be built, by reason alone, from scratch; that it was possible to sweep away all that had gone before and build an entirely new political system in its place, as if the old one never even existed. Burke, on the contrary, was a fallibilist about reason. He argued that the power of reason was limited: reason could not predict with certainty the outcome of decisions, and it could not alone provide the foundation for a working political system. Reason thus needed to be informed by tradition: we can only know what our political system should look like and what it should do, by working out what has worked in the past, and building upon that knowledge.

Burke also criticized the idea (common among Enlightenment thinkers) that the right to wield power is linked to reason and that, therefore, all reasoning beings should be considered able to wield power responsibly and justly. Burke was an elitist, and believed in the natural inequality of human beings. He disagreed with the defenders of the revolution that political power should be wielded by all individuals, and rejected, too, the idea that reason (disassociated from tradition) could reliably determine in advance where political power should lie. The principles arising out of reasoned reflection alone are too abstract and too indeterminate to yield sufficient answers to complicated questions about what should be done, and who should do it. Burke again believed that these questions were more concretely resolved by an appeal to tradition; history shows that some people are fit to rule and others are not. Burke thus believed that power should be located among those few – that is, the aristocracy – that history has shown to be endowed with the necessary qualities to wield it effectively, rather than indiscriminately doled out among the general population. This is a good example of conservative *pragmatism*. The idea is that politics should not be constrained by dogmatic ideological principle, but should instead be flexible enough to deal with the realities of each and every situation as it occurs in the real world: no one, not even the greatest philosophers the world has ever known, can work out from the comfort of their armchair who should govern and who should not; rather, these questions are best answered by working out who in any particular society has shown themselves most capable of wielding power effectively and responsibly and who has not. Burke's political views thus held three important implications. Firstly, a society characterized by class divisions and hierarchy rather than the liberal, Enlightenment vision of a society bound together by equals. Secondly, an elite system of representative government in which elected politicians govern on the basis of their own (superior) consciences and views, rather than the views of those who elected them. And thirdly, a conception of social and political change as necessarily gradualist, whereby social and political institutions develop over time, in increments, in response to developments in our knowledge of the world and in our experience of trying new things and applying those measures which work, and dropping those which do not.

We, therefore, see many ways in which Burke influenced Popper, and many ways in which he did not. Popper, of course, had little time for the idea that political rule should reside in a historical elite, or that it should be justified by the fact that some people are simply fit to rule while others are not. He also had little time for the idea of class. One of the central evils of historicism for Popper, we must remember, was that it was only interested in individual human beings in so far as they were members of *groups*: Marx was not interested so much in *people* as he was in *classes*, Hegel was not interested in *individuals* but rather in *nations*, and Plato's vision of the republic was characterized by a radical and unwavering class system (based on *race*). Popper, as we have seen, believed in the Enlightenment values of equality before the law and freedom of the individual. He also held with Enlightenment thinkers the idea that groups like class, nation, and race were arbitrary human constructs with little or no moral resonance, and that the genuine community to which we should be committed is the community of all human beings throughout the world. He therefore rejected claims made by conservatives like Burke that in order to justify change we must work out what would be in the best interests of the 'nation' or the 'community' or the 'group'. Popper believed such claims were characteristic of the closed society, rooted in outdated and pernicious ideas of historical fate, and exhibited the deliberate subordination of the interests of individual human beings to the interests of the groups or institutions of which they are members. If social and political reform was to be justi-fied, Popper believed, then it needed to be justified by, and to, those individuals who would bear the consequences of it. And because the ultimate and final consequences of any change cannot be predicted beforehand, any change must be cautious, responsible, and based on the best evidence we currently have. And if it turns out that a particular course of action was a mis-take, it must be reversible or changeable. Again, changes, and the justifications for them, must be considered *falsifiable*.

Popper believed in the capacity of individual human beings to improve their social and political lives by identifying problems and seeking solutions to them. But he was, like Burke, less optimistic than many Enlightenment thinkers about the power of reason to provide all the necessary information to construct new and complex political systems from scratch. He therefore believed, like Burke, that social reforms should be made on the basis of all the accumulated knowledge that the world currently possesses, and new institutions should grow out of those which already exist. While in the scientific realm it is appropriate for radical critique to bring about constant upheavals and shifts in thought, in the political realm, where lives are at stake, it is necessary to go more slowly, and to implement and explore changes gradually in a piecemeal fashion. Thus, Popper agreed with Burke's rejection of the French revolution, and argued, with Burke, against what he saw as the arrogant notion that all institutions should be understood as products of conscious human will. On the contrary, he united with Burke (and, as we will see, with Hayek) in suggesting that many social institutions are not 'created' but rather grow 'as the undesigned results of human actions' (Popper, 1957/2005; 59). But unlike Burke, Popper did not believe that the organic nature of these institutions justified or legitimated them. He did not defend the legitimacy of aristocratic rule, as Burke and others did; indeed, his political philosophy represents a direct challenge to any such theory. For Popper, political legitimacy was secured by testing existing institutions in their ability to achieve the ends afforded to them by the people, and in their ability to secure the social and political conditions necessary to allow such testing and public endorsement to occur. The idea that particular institutions or individuals should be rendered legitimate for reasons of historical precedent, or because they have always done so, was not merely anathema to Popper, but wrong and unjust. For Burke, tradition provided the justification of existing social and political conditions, including existing power structures, sources of authority, inequalities, and laws. For Popper, however, it represented a useful accumulation of (contestable) knowledge about the world, upon which reason might operate in order to provide guidance for piecemeal social reform.

For all their disagreements about equality, class, elitism, and the appropriate sources of authority, Popper and Burke were thus united in their rejection of radical change, and in their rejection of what they saw as blind faith on the part of other thinkers in the capacity of human reason to predict the outcome of events and decisions. Burke's fallibilism about reason led him to reject the Enlightenment aim of erecting free-standing conceptions of political life which were ahistorical and divorced from all that had gone before it. Popper sympathized, but also

pointed out the error in assuming that history alone could provide an alternative source of justification for political arrangements. Both thinkers thus acknowledged the limitations on
reason, although each drew different conclusions from it: Burke
used it to justify an appeal to historical tradition, while Popper
used it to ground his epistemological commitment to criticism
and critical rationalism. And both thinkers were more interested
in outlining the ways in which societies might appropriately
change, than in outlining a thoroughgoing vision of political life.
Neither Popper nor Burke were conservative in the simplistic
sense that they believed change was inherently bad. Change, for
Popper in particular, was not bad; after all, Popper's central
problem with Plato was that he aimed to suppress human creativity and freedom in order to 'arrest all change'. For Popper,
failing to change social or political institutions which are ineffi-
cient or unfit for purpose, or failing to reform social and political norms which are unjust, might prove disastrous. The point
for Popper (and for Burke) was to determine the appropriate
grounds on which change might be justified, and to work out
what *kind* of changes might be considered responsible. Although
he shared with Burke a rejection of the kind of changes justified
by utopianism, he embraced the capacity of individuals to
implement piecemeal reforms based on correct rational analysis
of existing and possible practices. Popper was specific about
what kind of institutions and policies we should *not* pursue (i.e.
historicist ones), but deliberately vague about what kind of
policies and institutions we *should* adopt, precisely because such
things could not be predicted in advance without collapsing
into utopian ideologism. Given that we cannot know for sure
the consequences of adopting particular policies or institutions
(even our favourite ones), we should avoid stipulating them in
too much detail at the outset, and secure instead the conditions
in which we might work out what institutions and policies would
best meet the identified needs of individual members of society
at any one time.

Radical politics, radical philosophy

In the years following World War II, conservatism had begun to take on a broader meaning, and many writers – who had little or no relation to Burke's classical conservatism – were labelled conservative. This process of re-labelling was largely driven by their critics. The debate as to whether Popper was or was not a conservative, for example, has been largely driven by his critics, primarily from the Left, who have interpreted his commitment to individualism and a broadly market-oriented economy as representing establishment views, and exhibiting an unwillingness to challenge the ideological dominance of liberal capitalism. Although in many respects *The Open Society* represented a powerful statement of the social democratic consensus that had reigned in Europe since World War II, Popper was nevertheless lumped together with other 'cold war liberals' like Isaiah Berlin and Raymon Aron who defended liberal individualism and markets in the face of communism in the 1950s. Berlin in particular shared Popper's concerns about the encroaching threat of totalitarianism, and identified the same enemies to democracy as Popper; his inaugural lecture (and most famous essay) 'Two Concepts of Liberty' traced the philosophical roots of totalitarianism to those thinkers like Hegel, Marx, and Rousseau who had defended a 'positive' account of liberty, and others essays including 'Historical Inevitability' bore all the hallmarks of Popper's work.

During the 1960s and 1970s, Popper was considered hopelessly out of date by many on the Left for remaining committed to a *politics* of individualism rather than embracing the radical politics of social movements and protest, and a *philosophy* of enlightenment through critique and rational reflection. His continued defence of liberalism, gradualism, and the futility of radical planning at a time when so many inside and outside the academy were turning towards a more 'progressive' collectivist politics premised upon radical social change put him in the conservative camp. Critics suggested that the many of the ills that beset British and American society, for example, were too important and ingrained in prevailing ideals to be tackled tentatively in a piecemeal fashion. The American civil rights movement and the campaign for women's rights, for example, both embodied a political will to tackle fundamental problems quickly, and to take direct action which bypassed the usual channels, which many believed were the source of the problem itself. Popper's 'institutional approach' and his appeal to political gradualism through piecemeal social engineering appeared reactionary and seemed to set him against those who fought for important rights and equalities. His claim that responsible change was tentative and gradual, the implicit assumption that people should not step outside of conventional democratic debates in the interests of affecting change, and that people should work with existing institutions rather than against them seemed to suggest that campaigners for civil rights and others causes were making a mistake in speaking out against the status quo, and should raise their concerns more reasonably, through those channels which had shown themselves to be effective. Similarly, his claim that all knowledge claims are necessarily conjectural struck many as a capitulation to existing social and political injustices; while the certainty of some claims may well be questionable, they conceded, can we not know for certain that, for example, women are equal to men? Or that black people should not be denied the rights possessed by white people? Or that gays and lesbians should not be intimidated or forced to hide their sexuality for fear of ostracism or abuse?

Central to the radicalism which characterized politics at that time was a sense that, for all their claims to be on the side of all individuals equally, traditional liberal democratic political institutions and mechanisms prioritized the voices (and hence, the interests) of mainstream majorities over those of minority groups. That is, behind the liberal rhetoric of equal treatment, freedom, individuality, and the capacity of all individuals to participate fully and meaningfully in the political process, traditional liberal democratic politics merely enshrined what Mill called the 'tyranny of the majority'. Many felt that more needed to be done for those gays and lesbians, black people, immigrants, and others whose interests were being systematically over-ridden by the majority. Their answer was a new politics of identity, of social movements and protest; a recognition of the fact that if members of marginalized groups spoke together as one voice, that voice would ring louder than if they all spoke separately. The answer, then, was a rejection of traditional individualism, and of the conventional liberal concern for all those things which *distinguished* individuals from one another, in place of a new emphasis on those things which *united* people, and a rejection of traditional deference to existing social and political institutions, in place of a radical anti-establishment counter-culture. In place of a rather abstract, Enlightenment conception of politics rooted in individuality and reason, the new activism emphasized shared identity, community, and the idea that persons could be bound together by more than a commitment to liberal principles and critical rationalism: things like shared culture, or race, or ethnicity, or gender. Liberals had traditionally considered such distinctions to be pernicious and irrelevant: something to be transcended. Popper agreed. But the new activism suggested that they could be sources of great social and political unity and strength and, in the context of majoritarian liberal democratic states, a means of bringing about social changes which mere individualism could never do.

Many critics therefore suggested that for all Popper's high-sounding talk in *The Open Society* of equality and the importance of open debate among political equals, his stubborn commitment to individualist politics and his rejection of the importance of social groups (as a throwback to the tribal politics of the closed society) represented little more than a description of the problem itself: a political system which prided itself on breaking down the barriers which separated people but which, in practice, was exclusionary and elitist, by placing de facto power in the hands of the majority. This problem was only exacerbated by the vision of democratic deliberation upon which Popper built his theory. Premised as it was on his wider epistemological claims that knowledge grew out the dynamic process of conjecture and refutation, critique, and trial and error, many wondered how such a political vision could ever hope to yield the kind of agreement and consensus necessary in politics. What Popper seemed to envisage was a society which evolved slowly on the basis of a tradition of rationalist critique, but which was characterized by ceaseless debate, refutation, conjecture, the proposal of bold political initiatives, and their subsequent falsification. But, critics pointed out, there is more to democracy than talking. For a democracy to function effectively, it needs to be able to make decisions, to act, on the basis of reasonable agreements among citizens, lawmakers, and politicians. The concern – which we find in its most radical form in thinkers like Carl Schmitt – is that democratic debate becomes disassociated from democratic decision-making, and that while the people discuss issues amongst themselves, the most important decisions are in fact made behind the scenes (Schmitt, 1923/1988, and 1927/2006). Popper's idealized conception of a deliberative democracy was thus seen by many socialists and progressives sympathetic to collectivism and the politics of identity to both *exclude* marginalized groups from the democratic process and to *disassociate* democratic debate from the process of political decision-making. Thus it was seen by these people as a de facto argument for elite rule, and a blueprint for conservatism.

Moreover, Popper's unwavering commitment to the 'narratives' of individual freedom and critical rationalism seemed naïve and simplistic to many on the Left who were increasingly falling under the influence of European critical theorists like Adorno, Horkheimer, Habermas, and Marcuse, and of poststructuralists like Foucault. Popper's philosophical approach was squarely in the analytical tradition of Russell and Ayer; his critique of Marx was thus an analytical one, in which he tried to replace Marx's universalism with a universalism of his own, a liberal universalism rooted in individual freedom. Although very different in other ways, postmodernists, poststructuralists, and the critical theorists of the Frankfurt School were broadly united in their rejection of such an enterprise as grounded in meta-narratives of modernity which were no longer tenable, and appealing to concepts, ideals, and values which had lost their meaning. Critical theorists like Habermas accused Popper of being merely a positivist: his critique of Marx, and his vision of the open society – indeed, his entire approach to philosophy – was seen as merely an expression of bourgeois ideology, too bound up in its own partial understanding of the world to capture anything important about it, and too quick to reach for 'universal' principles which were not universal at all (Habermas, 1976). For his radical critics, Popper's broad claim that it was possible for individuals to identify and resolve problems in so many different realms of human experience in the same way, according to the same process and method, was naïve, and placed far too much faith in the ability of one conception of reasoning to reveal all the hidden and significant intricacies of the natural world, social life, politics, power, freedom, and everything else. Hence, they believed that his approach actually *limited* the growth of knowledge; it missed entirely the fact that the concepts we use to understand ourselves and the world, the language we use to communicate with one another and to express these concepts are problematic, ambiguous, indeterminate, and increasingly out of kilter with the world in which they were used.

Most importantly of all, for the critical theorists and poststructuralists, Popper's argument failed to say anything about the most important thing about politics: the nature and location of power, and the explicit and implicit ways in which power is exercised in liberal democratic states. While Popper accepted Marx's dictum that 'it is not the consciousness of men that determines their being, but, on the contrary, their social being that determines their consciousness' undermined psychologism, he refused to draw the same conclusion from it as the Marxists.

For the critical theorists and poststructuralists, Marx's claim that one's social, political, and economic environment can shape one's thoughts, interests, and understandings reveals the important ways in which one's social environment can represent a source of coercion. Having rejected this claim as the 'conspiracy theory' of society, Popper was able to discuss power in the traditional liberal manner, namely, as something that was possessed by the state, and which needed to be limited or constrained by laws and policies rooted in a respect for individual rights. But the critical theorists and poststructuralists argued that Marx's claims could not be so easily dismissed, and that, once we understand that one's interests and thoughts might be shaped (sometimes subtly, sometimes implicitly, in ways that we may or may not even notice) by society *itself*, rather than by particular *people* or *institutions*, then liberal arguments about individual freedom and rights simply miss the point. The aim of politics should not be merely to work out how – and to what extent – state power should be limited, and hence, what constitutional and legal safeguards need to be in place in order to protect the individual from it (as it is in liberal theory), but rather, to reveal the many ways in which power is exerted through those social and political norms which regulate our behaviour on a daily basis, to reveal who has the power to shape and determine these social norms, and suggest ways in which these dominant and insidious power structures might be broken down.

This key insight is one shared by many thinkers who do not otherwise belong among the poststructuralist or critical theory camp. Feminists in particular have criticized, and continue to criticize, the kind of Enlightenment reasoning implicit in liberal theory, and which are evident in Popper's ideas about society and the growth of knowledge. Feminists including, most recently, Seyla Benhabib, Nancy Fraser, Nancy Hirschmann, and Iris Marion Young have drawn upon poststructuralist insights in their work in order to suggest that the traditional liberal conception of power (as something which is embodied in, and can be regulated in, the public sphere) cannot explain the myriad ways in which women in particular are controlled and oppressed in the private realm, and hence, cannot form the basis of an egalitarian response to patriarchy (Benhabib, 1992; Fraser, 1997; Hirschmann, 2003; Young, 1990). The principle source of women's oppression, many feminists have argued, is not the state, but the implicit power structures embodied in the norms which regulate those relationships which liberals take to be private: the relationships between husbands and wives, for example, or mothers and children, or the norms embodied in religious or other communities of which women are members. Popper was, as we have seen, deeply sceptical of the idea that individuals are 'controlled' by their social and political circumstances in the sense that their choices (and their capacity for choice itself) are somehow shaped or thwarted by society. But it is not enough to say that such claims represent a conspiracy theory promulgated by people who use pretentious words and long, impenetrable sentences (as he did). Popper's theory provides little help in addressing this issue, other than to say that we should understand all individuals as equals regardless of gender, and discuss the problem. It says nothing about the deeper claim that many women will feel unable to engage in public deliberation, or in anything else, as free and equal individuals as a result of power structures which are invisible in Popper's philosophy, but which nevertheless serve to undermine the freedom of women to make genuinely free choices about their lives. Popper's rejection of what he calls the conspiracy theory of power in this and other contexts is, for many theorists, simply further evidence of his unwillingness to recognize the importance of groups, and the norms which characterize them.

In the face of such a radical and fundamental critique of modern society, of liberalism, and of the way in which we understand our concepts and language, then, Popper's belief that social problems can be overcome by asserting individual freedom and open dialogue seemed conservative indeed. Popper argued that change could not be radical, and that 'social experiments' should not be conducted at the level of society as a whole; he argued that we should adopt a methodologically individualist and nominalist approach to understanding society, rather than a holistic, collectivist, and organic one, given the inability of either reason or history to provide certain guides to the future development of humankind. But poststructuralists and critical theorists suggested that it is possible to be a fallibilist about reason while at the same time adopting a radical approach to understanding and resolving social and political problems. Popper argued that social scientists needed to choose between two opposing approaches to understanding society: one which acknowledged the limited capacity of reason to reveal certain knowledge about the long-term future by adopting a piecemeal approach to reforming society (and which presupposed the central importance of critique and a broadly liberal conception of individual freedom), and one which sought to understand societies in a holistic, collectivist way, and which presupposed the capacity of historical laws to determine the future development of humankind. Postmodernists, poststructuralists and critical theorists on the other hand, appeared to provide a third approach: one which shared the historicist commitment to holism and collectivism, and shared too Popper's scepticism about the power of reason to produce certain knowledge of the future. A common theme in critical theory and poststructuralism was and is that only by radically deconstructing the language and concepts embodied in any social and political system will we understand the ways in which power is exercised within it, and the ends to which this power is exerted. Rather than stand aloof from society and its most insidious problems, then, we should seek a deep understanding of these things, and of the social whole, in order to reveal those injustices which afflict the lives of individuals, shape their experiences, and yet often remain hidden. *Contra* Popper, the postmodernists, poststructuralists, and the critical theorists argued, in their own ways, that social and political science is necessarily and unavoidably radical; understanding society involves a radical engagement with its institutions, its history, and the people who compose it, and resolving its problems requires acting upon what we find. And what we find will not always respond well to piecemeal, tentative reform, but must be resolved instead by initiatives which have far-reaching, and possibly revolutionary, implications.

Popper's response to these criticisms – in as much as he responded at all – was not to give ground, but to further entrench his commitment to individualism and democratic dialogue. His political writings following *The Open Society* were characterized by a dogged support of liberal democratic virtues over those of other systems; liberal democracy is, he said, 'by far the best society which has come into existence during the course of human history . . . the best there has ever been – the best, at least, of which we have any historical knowledge' (Popper, 1963/2007b, 496). In response to those which suggested that his vision of the open society was too abstract and empty of the kind of substantive values which could unite the citizenry, Popper increasingly characterized critical rationalism as a substantive *tradition* to which people could subscribe without falling into tribalism (Popper, 1963/2007b). And in his 1965 essay 'The Myth of the Framework', Popper railed against the relativism at the heart of poststructuralism and critical theory. A few years earlier, in his contribution to what has become known as the Positivism Debate, Popper poured withering scorn on the theorists of the Frankfurt School. In response to Habermas's charge that Popper was merely a positivist, 'bound by his methodology to defend the status-quo' (Popper, 1994a; 68), Popper pointed out – not unreasonably – that he had devoted his career to refuting the positivism characteristic of the Vienna Circle. He also described the influence of the Frankfurt School as 'irrationalist and 'intelligence-destroying', and claimed that he was unable to 'take their methodology (whatever that might mean) seriously from either an intellectual or scholarly point of view' (Popper, 1994a; 66). They were, he said, like Hegel, caught up in a 'cult of incomprehensibility' which was both self-indulgent and irresponsible. Habermas, for example, did 'not know how to put things simply, clearly, and modestly', indeed, Popper felt, most of what he had to say was either trivial or mistaken. Adorno, he felt, had 'nothing whatever to say' and defended a philosophical vision that was merely 'mumbo-jumbo' (Popper, 1994a; 78). Similarly, Horkheimer's work was, he believed, 'empty', 'devoid of content', 'uninteresting', and 'merely a vague and unoriginal form of Marxian historicism' (Popper, 1994a; 79–80).

The charge of incomprehensibility was not, for Popper, superficial. Popper, we must recall, believed that the growth of knowledge depended upon critical debate across disciplines; hence, it was, he thought, the *moral responsibility* of anyone committed to the growth of knowledge to aim for accessibility and clarity in their work, so as to avoid being understandable only by a small group of like-minded intellectuals. In deliberately making their theories as complex as possible, Popper believed, the critical theorists and poststructuralists were doing little more than feed their own vanity and arrogance, and placing limits on the pursuit of knowledge. 'The total content of the so-called Critical Theory of the Frankfurt School,' Popper claimed, was thus: 'Let the present generation suffer and perish – for all we can do is to expose the ugliness of the world we live in, and to heap insults on our oppressors, the "bourgeoisie"' (Popper, 1994a; 84). Popper, on the other hand, argued for the possibility of reforming society for the better. 'We can do much more *now* to relieve suffering and, most importantly, to increase freedom', he said. 'We must not wait for a goddess of history or a goddess of revolution to introduce better conditions into human affairs' (Popper, 1994a; 80) as the critical theorists counselled. To emphasize the inability of human beings to understand the world in the face of incommensurable linguistic and cultural 'frameworks', and to systematically undermine our ability to change the world in which we live was, for Popper, a betrayal and a mistake, and belonged to the very same tradition of arrogant philosophical elitism that he identified, and rejected, in the coffee houses of his native Vienna. For critical theorists like Adorno, Horkheimer and Marcuse, for whom the deeply problematic nature of apparently simple concepts was precisely the point, Popper's response fell wide of the mark.

Popper and the rise of the New Right

By the late 1970s and early 1980s, the meaning of conservatism in public and academic discourse shifted still further. Popper claimed that one of his principal aims in writing *The Open Society* was to unite the trade unions and socialists behind the idea that totalitarianism had replaced capitalism as the main threat facing the world. By the 1980s, however, Popper's ideas would provide a rallying point for a very different political agenda. For many British and American liberals and conservatives during the 1960s and 1970s, the enemy was not merely the totalitarianism which had grown overseas, or domestic radicalism and counter-cultural movements, but the *collectivism* which had infiltrated the politics of Europe and the US. The roots of this collectivism lay in the broadly social democratic consensus established in the years immediately following World War II, many elements of which were articulated in *The Open Society*. Post-war Europe was focused on rebuilding the shattered societies and economies of European states. The state took a much more central role in the redistribution of wealth and the provision of welfare than it had previously done under liberalism, and there was a general sense among politicians and the wider society that the politics of the time called for a strengthening of unity and solidarity over individualism and competition.

Many of the ideas which characterized this consensus remained, and were strengthened, in the years between 1945 and the late 1970s. In Britain, for example, successive governments remained hospitable to a broadly social democratic programme emphasizing the public provision of welfare, state intervention in the economy, and the extension of the state into areas such as housing and the ownership of utilities. The drive to create jobs and to rebuild industry resulted in a strengthened labour movement represented by increasingly powerful trade unions. Increasingly dominant, then, was the idea that it was in some sense a responsibility of government to promote social unity through state action, to take seriously those things which bound people together (into a labour movement, into a class, into a people), and that it was possible for the state to engage in planned reform of society. For liberals, committed to free markets, individualism, and limited politics, and conservatives, committed to pragmatism, tradition, and a profound anti-socialism (or, more accurately, a profound anti-radicalism which seemed at odds with socialism), the continued move towards collectivism was a cause for concern. Consequently, despite their many differences, liberals and conservatives increasingly found themselves speaking as one voice against what they saw as the twin evils of collectivism and radical (i.e. ideological) social engineering. Fears that the state was engaging in unrealistic social engineering, and that politics was becoming too dominated by powerful groups like the trade unions reached a crisis point in the late 1970s. At that time – a period of considerable social, political, and economic unrest – many liberals and conservatives thought that things had gone far enough. The state was seen to have over-stepped its bounds, it had become too unwieldy to make good on its reform plans; it had spread itself too thin – sought to get involved in too many aspects of peoples' lives – and, as a consequence, had acceded too much power to the trade unions and other sectional interest groups. Liberals and conservatives thus united under the banner of the 'New Right', and argued for an alternative: a return to political pragmatism, limited politics, individualism, and the freeing of the individual from the burden of a meddlesome, intrusive state. And they did so by turning to the economic and political theory of Popper's long-time friend and colleague Friedrich von Hayek.

Hayek, as we saw in Chapter 1, was a great admirer of Popper's work, and was instrumental in the publication of *The Open Society* and Popper's move to the LSE in 1946. Popper, in return, claimed that Hayek 'saved his life', and described him as a father-figure and his intellectual superior. Hayek was also the intellectual inspiration behind the New Right, and has been widely credited as the single most important figure in the resurgence of *laissez-faire* economics in Britain and the US. Popper and Hayek shared more than merely friendship: they were contemporaries, driven by a united concern for individual freedom and a rejection of tyranny, and their ideas were rooted in the same motivating philosophy: that 'man does not and cannot know everything, and when he acts as if he does, disaster follows' (Blundell, 1999; 12). Both Popper and Hayek were united in their rejection of the kind of radical change which characterized the French revolution, and were united with Burke in their support of a particular brand of philosophical rationalism in its place. Both rejected the overly optimistic view (typified by thinkers like Bacon) that reason – disassociated from tradition and theory – was capable of revealing certain and fundamental truths about the world, and hence, both united with Burke in his broad claim that a functioning political system could not be dreamed up by reason alone. '[T]he pessimists who feared the decline of authority and tradition were wise men', Popper argued. 'The terrible experience of the great religious wars, and of the French and Russian revolutions, prove their wisdom and foresight' (Popper, 1963/2007b; 503).

Popper, Burke, and Hayek were thus united with other thinkers like Bernard Mandeville, Adam Smith, and David Hume in adopting what Hayek called an 'evolutionary rationalism' over a 'constructivist' one: a form of rationalism, which acknowledged the value of accumulated wisdom and tradition in reasoning about social and political reform, rather than ahistorical, abstract theorizing (Mandeville, 1714; Smith, 1789; Hume, 1748). While constructivist rationalists – including such diverse figures as Descartes, Rousseau, and Condorcet in France, to Bacon, Hobbes, and defenders of the French revolution like Godwin, Paine, and Jefferson in Britain and America – emphasized the ability of humankind to 'sweep away existing institutions and practices and propose the adoption of completely new, untried plans', evolutionary rationalists counselled caution (Gamble, 1996; 32). An important task of philosophy, for Hayek and for Popper, was to discover the limits of reason and to determine the appropriate means of structuring and reforming society in circumstances of epistemological uncertainty. Importantly, then, it was not to replace *rationalism* with *traditionalism* (that is, to replace the uncritical optimism about reason with an unquestioned appreciation of historical tradition, as thinkers like Oakeshott argued), but rather to construct an idea of rationalism which was attentive to the wisdom embodied in tradition, but which allowed for the fact that such wisdom could not be certain or unequivocal. Hayek called this *evolutionary* rationalism, Popper called it *critical* rationalism, and it is what many believe puts them both in the same conservative tradition as Burke. Such an approach enshrined Popper's fundamental claim (discussed in the previous chapter), that knowledge often begins in *myths* and *traditions* as much as it begins in reason and, hence, it

> makes room . . . for a reconciliation between rationalism and traditionalism. The critical rationalist can appreciate traditions, for although he believes in truth, he does not believe that he himself is in certain possession of it. He can appreciate every step, every approach towards it, as valuable, indeed as invaluable; and he can see that our traditions often help to encourage such steps, and also that without an intellectual tradition the individual could hardly take a single step towards the truth. It is thus the critical approach to rationalism, the compromise between rationalism and scepticism, which for a long time has been the basis of the British middle way: the respect for traditions, and at the same time, the recognition of the need to reform them. (Popper, 1963/2007b; 505)

For Hayek, as for Popper, the inability of reason to provide certainty, and hence, to be capable of predicting with precision the future consequences of any particular action or decision, underwrote a political programme which rejected not only radical change but also long-term economic and social planning, in favour of piecemeal progress through trial and error.

While the similarities between the two authors – and with the New Right in general – are clear, it is more difficult to determine exactly how *influential* Popper's work was to Hayek's critique of radicalism, and social, economic, and political planning. In 1982, Hayek claimed that 'ever since [Popper's] *Logik der Forschung* first came out in 1934, I have been a complete adherent to his general philosophy of methodology' (Weimer & Palermo, 1982; 323). He also believed that Popper's terminology would appeal to Leftists who were deaf to Hayek himself. Milton Friedman, another leading light of the New Right, suggested the adoption of Popper's theory of falsification into economics. Hayek, like Popper, argued against the tendency to split the search for knowledge into exclusive disciplines; like Popper, Hayek criticized conservatives for down playing the pursuit of knowledge (in case they discovered something that held implications that they did not like); and, like Popper, Hayek criticized conservatives and others for supporting a nationalist approach to economic policy, rather than an internationalist, cosmopolitan one. Both Hayek and Popper refused to be pigeonholed as supporters of any particular ideology. Neither thinker believed that they were in the business of peddling a particular ideological position, rather, they both felt that their ideas cut across ideologies – *transcended* them – by presenting a series of claims about knowledge and freedom which were *descriptive* rather than *normative*. Neither Hayek nor Popper claimed to be presenting a 'liberal' understanding of knowledge, rather, they claimed to be merely describing how knowledge actually does in fact grow, what can be said about it, and what we one might appropriately do with it. Having done so, both converged on liberalism (broadly conceived) as the doctrine most able to function in circumstances of epistemological uncertainty.

Nevertheless, Popper and Hayek disagreed over what liberalism entailed. In particular they disagreed over the appropriate extent of state intervention in social and economic matters. Popper's general political vision, after all, was social democratic. He was highly critical of what he called 'unrestrained capitalism', calling it 'inhumane' and 'unjust'. In *The Open Society*, for example, Popper explicitly stated that his view had 'nothing to do with the policy of strict non-intervention (often, but not quite accurately called *laissez-faire*). Liberalism and state interference are not opposed to on another' (Popper, 1945/2006a; 117). Popper argued strongly that unregulated free markets and *laissez-faire* economics violated, rather than protected, individual freedom by failing to protect the economically weak from the economically strong. 'Even if the state protects its citizens from being bullied by physical violence (as it does, in principle, under the system of unrestrained capitalism),' Popper stated, 'it may defeat our ends by its failure to protect them from the misuse of economic power . . . [U]nlimited economic freedom can be just as self-defeating as unlimited physical freedom, and economic power may be nearly as dangerous as physical violence' (Popper, 1945/2006b; 135).

Consequently, he argued, the 'principle of non-intervention, of an unrestrained economic system [of the kind advocated by Hayek and Friedman], has to be given up. If we wish freedom to be safeguarded, then we must demand that the policy of unlimited economic freedom be replaced by the planned economic intervention of the state. We must demand that unrestrained capitalism give way to an economic interventionism' (Popper, 1945/2006b; 135–6). Such a project was entirely consistent with his rejection of utopianism, or so he thought. We can, for example, 'develop a rational political programme for the protection of the economically weak' without collapsing into utopianism. 'We can', for example, 'make laws to limit exploitation. We can limit the working day . . . [W]e can insure the workers (or better, all citizens) against disability, unemployment, and old age. In this way, we can make impossible such forms of exploitation as are based on the helpless economic position of a worker who must yield to anything in order not to starve . . . Economic power', he went on, 'must not be permitted to dominate political power; if necessary, it must be fought and brought under control by political power' (Popper, 1945/2006b; 136–7). Similarly, he argued, it is also 'the responsibility of the state to see that its citizens are given an education enabling them to participate in the life of the community, and to make use of any opportunity to develop their interests and gifts' irrespective of their ability to pay (Popper, 1945/2006a; 139). 'A certain amount of state control in education . . . is necessary, if the young are to be protected from a neglect which would make them unable to defend their freedom, and the state should see that all educational facilities are available to everybody' (Popper, 1945/2006a; 117–18).

The fact that intervention 'will tend to increase the power of the state . . . is extremely dangerous . . . [but] not a decisive argument against it', Popper believed (Popper, 1945/2006b; 141). Intervention must be accompanied by a strengthening of democratic institutions, and it should always be informed by his negative utilitarianism, that is, in the pursuit of fighting 'concrete evils rather than to establish some ideal good. State intervention should be limited to what is really necessary for the protection of individual freedom', namely, the establishment and reform of social and political institutions which encourage free debate among citizens, and which are capable of enacting piecemeal reforms based upon past experience and knowledge. Hayek disagreed, arguing that epistemological uncertainty invalidated *any* attempt at social, economic, or political planning.

Popper's politics cannot be understood to be wholly conservative, then, but rather as containing elements which influenced, and were influenced by, conservatism. Similarly, his views can obviously be seen to have influenced libertarian thinkers, but they do not fit easily in this tradition either. Libertarianism has been particularly influential in the US, through thinkers like Ayn Rand and Robert Nozick, who argued for a reduction in the size and scope of the state in order to establish for all individuals as significant a realm of private choice as possible, free from coercion, and a general support for individualism, the minimal state, and private property rights (Nozick, 1974; Rand, 1943). But also powerful in libertarianism are the themes of experimentation and risk; of change and, in particular, the capacity of free individuals to exert their will on society in ways which bring about new and innovative ways of doing things which are often profound and radical breaks with the past. These themes seem controversial with regard to both Popper and Hayek, both of whom were sceptical of radical change and risky social reforms. Indeed, Hayek was sceptical of American libertarianism for precisely this reason: that it seemed to be rooted in a constructivist account of rationality rather than an evolutionary one, and as such fell into the same trap of exalting reason over tradition as the Russian and French revolutionaries (Gamble, 1996). Popper shared this concern and, like Hayek, also sought to defend the importance of tradition in politics and society: libertarianism seemed wedded to a vision of society as united only by the self-interest of its individual members. Popper – perhaps in partial response to his radical critics – increasingly emphasized the role of tradition in uniting individuals together. Also, it is crucially important to distinguish between Popper's methodology (his epistemology) and the political/practical outcomes yielded by this epistemology. His epistemology was very radical, and appeared in line with a broadly libertarian view. The development of human knowledge in the realms of science as well as politics emerges out of the often 'reckless' pursuit of truth by individual human beings who, on the whole, attempt to impose order on the world and their lives by trying to explain them. Ideas rise and fall in an ongoing process of critique and rational reflection, rather like companies in a market economy: 'Science, and more specifically scientific progress', he argued, 'are the results not of isolated efforts, but of the free competition of thought' (Popper, 1957/2005; 143). Theories that are able to withstand the rigors of intellectual competition remain candidates for the truth, those which are not, are abandoned. However, the practical outcome of this dynamic process is, in fact, political gradualism. Societies should develop slowly, as a consequence of many piecemeal challenges and interventions made by individual human beings all making their own way in the world, against a background of existing knowledge and tradition. He believed that people should be free to make their own mistakes and take risks – indeed, the growth of knowledge depends upon such people. But he did not believe that the state should justify social reforms on such a basis. Social and political reform needed to be tentative, gradual, and risk-averse, not radical and risky.

A final word on ideologies

It is ironic that Popper's political vision, articulated in *The Open Society* and various later essays, represented a powerful defence of the social democratic consensus that had reigned in Europe from 1945 to the 1970s, yet was used by people who called themselves libertarians, liberals, and conservatives to destroy precisely that consensus. Despite arguing for the role of limited social planning and state intervention in the economy, Popper's epistemology, filtered through Hayek and Friedman, provided the philosophical backdrop to the rise of the New Right and the destruction of political collectivism. He advocated the redistribution of wealth and the public provision of welfare in order to protect the economically weak from the economically strong, but his ideas were widely praised by world leaders including Margaret Thatcher (who described him as her favourite philosopher), and entrepreneurs like George Soros, who has amassed a personal fortune by investing on global markets according to Popperian principles. He was, for much of his life, a socialist; he continued to respect Marx, and shared his rejection of *laissez-faire* economics, but rejected the left-wing politics of the 1960s and 1970s, and paved the way for its destruction in the 1980s. He joined many Enlightenment thinkers in celebrating the capacity of human beings to change the world for the better, but joined with critics of the Enlightenment in rejecting the notion (found among liberal and socialist revolutionaries) that reason could justify radical change.

Popper's views do not fit easily in any particular ideological camp, and so we should not try to make them. Popper himself had little time for labels, and did not engage much in debates about which camp he most appropriately belonged to. His anti-essentialism meant that he had little interest in engaging in discussions about the meaning of terms like 'conservatism' or 'libertarianism', and his antipathy towards breaking up the pursuit of knowledge into distinct disciplines or methodologies meant that he cared little for the activity of demarcating boundaries among ideas such that they form distinct ideological positions. There is some sense in this. The desire by critics and supporters to squash complex thinkers like Popper into fixed ideological positions inevitably leads to a simplification and misrepresentation of their views; people who choose to call themselves conservatives or liberals or libertarians may wish to claim Popper for themselves, but in doing so they would have to conveniently forget those often pivotal aspects of his theory which were inconsistent with their wider ideals. Popper was rightly sceptical of such an endeavour, and of the stifling consequences it had on the growth of knowledge. We might do well, when thinking about the Popper's rightful place in the history of political thought, to adopt a Popperian approach: to abandon the search for the ideological 'essence' of Popper's views (and the attendant desire to label him one thing or the other), and instead to engage with his ideas, and to attempt to defeat them through reasonable and rigorous deliberation and debate.

4

The Contemporary Relevance of Popper's Philosophy

In many ways, reading Popper's work is like peering through a window into another time: a time in which liberal democracy was under threat from totalitarianism, and individual freedom, equality, and rights were being threatened by the primal, collectivist politics of Nazism, Stalinism, and Fascism; a time in which the cosmopolitan quest for the international unity of all peoples under principles of reason and progress was being challenged by the strident forces of nationalism and war. As a philosophical and political work, *The Open Society* is very much a child of its time: animated by a strident belief in individual freedom over tyranny, and informed by a commitment to the Enlightenment values of science, logic, and reason over what Popper saw as the mysticism and exclusionary implications of philosophical idealism. And, together with *The Poverty of Historicism*, it represents a statement about society – and the *study* of society – which is rooted in a particular historical moment, but no particular political ideology.

Popper's claims concerning epistemology, society, and politics are not merely historical artefacts, however. They represent genuine contributions to social and political thought which possess an enduring significance. Popper's political philosophy represents a bold and controversial vision of what politics can and cannot achieve, and what politicians, philosophers, and social scientists should or should not do. Nevertheless, Popper's work is often neglected among contemporary political theorists, and Anglo-American political theorists in particular. It is entirely possible, and perhaps normal, for a student to gain a degree in politics without having ever studied Popper. Undergraduate courses in political theory rarely have a week on Popper, and Popper's political works are often neglected by more mainstream philosophers who – if they are interested in Popper at all – are more concerned with his theories about the philosophy of the natural sciences. One possible reason for this, perhaps, is the view that Popper's political works have been eclipsed by political events. Popper began work on *The Open Society and Its Enemies* in 1938, when Hitler invaded his native Austria. At that time, fascism and communism were more than merely interesting philosophical puzzles to investigate – they were dominant forces in world politics, united by a commitment to centralize power in an elite class of leaders who claimed to know the interests of the people better than the people themselves ever could, and committed to using this knowledge as a justification for subjugation and tyranny. Following the defeat of Nazism in World War II, and, later, the dissolution of the Soviet Union in the 1980s and early 1990s, these threats all but disappeared from the world stage, leaving many to feel, perhaps, that Popper's dissection of their motivating philosophies was redundant.

If this *is* the reason for Popper's neglect among contemporary political philosophers, then it is a mistake. The redundancy of Popper's critique of totalitarianism and historicism in politics is overstated, and his rejection of the closed society continues to hold important implications for contemporary politics. For while Nazism and Fascism are indeed in retreat, global politics is still cursed with many of the evils that Popper railed against. The tribalism characteristic of the closed society is still all too evident in the ethnic and nationalist conflicts which continue to blight so much of the world, and in the increased politicization and radicalization of religion in so many countries, including those governed by liberal democratic institutions. Despite increasingly popular claims among many social and political scientists, practitioners and commentators about the erosion of national and ethnic identities in the wake of globalization, increased migration, and the spread of capitalist markets, and of the decline in the political significance of the nation state as a consequence of the rise in supranational institutions like the IMF, the World Bank, the EU, and the UN, the willingness among many people to cling to cultural or religious or ethnic identities, to fight for them, and to kill in their name seems as strong as ever. Similarly, the willingness of undemocratic leaders and regimes to use the institutions of the state to brutalize their citizens, to tyrannize them, and to deny them basic freedoms, all in the name of some greater good, represents an enduring source of misery for hundreds of thousands of people throughout the world. The open society still has enemies. They may be different to the ones that Popper wrote about, but Popper's critique of fascism and totalitarianism applies as directly and coherently to the newer, more obvious evils of religious fanaticism, authoritarianism, and nationalism that we see around us today.

Popper's political philosophy, above all else, represents a vindication of liberalism, democracy, and reason over tribalism, authoritarianism, and tyranny; it represents a strident defence of the right of each and every individual in the world not to live in fear of those who govern them, to be involved in decisions about the future direction of their political community, and to live a life that they feel to be worthwhile, freely and without unjust constraint. It therefore represents a defence of cosmopolitan individualism in the face of those in or outside of the academy who argue that political institutions should affirm or give special recognition to claims arising out of religious, ethnic, cultural, or nationalist identity. Such claims have become increasingly popular not just among certain political regimes, but among political philosophers too. The question of how states (and citizens) should respond to cultural, ethnic, and religious diversity has become incredibly important in recent years, especially among decision-makers in the US, and in European states like Britain and the Netherlands. The extent to which minority groups should be required to assimilate to the prevailing values of the majority, and how liberal states should manage the balance between respecting minority identities while encouraging common values in all individuals regardless of their particular beliefs and ideals remains incredibly vexed and controversial, and a source of deep disagreement among policy-makers, parliamentarians, and practitioners. Contemporary political philosophy, too, has been dominated in recent years by a resurgent interest among political theorists (both within and outside the liberal tradition) in the importance of particularist identities within liberal democratic politics. Certain liberal theorists like Will Kymlicka (1997) and Joseph Raz (1986; 1996), liberal nationalists like David Miller (1995) and Yael Tamir (1993), communitarians like Michael Sandel (1982) and Alasdair MacIntyre (1996), difference theorists like Iris Marion Young (1990) and Nancy Fraser (1997), and many others besides have argued for the philosophical, moral, and normative significance of communities and groups in liberal democratic politics, and have, in their own ways, criticized what they see as the naïve and abstract individualism at the heart of traditional liberal political thought. Popper's social and political philosophy represents a coherent and enduring counter-argument to such a move, but it is one which is hardly ever mentioned or discussed. Some theorists have suggested that the establishment of a common politics among diverse groups is impossible because many of the values embodied in these groups will be incommensurable with one another and, hence, there will be no common ground over which different groups can communicate (e.g. Gray, 2000). Others have argued for a form of political pluralism which acknowledges the sometimes incompatible needs of different groups (e.g. Parekh, 2005). Popper shares with contemporary political liberals like John Rawls (1993) and Charles Larmore (2008), and difference theorists like Iris Marion Young (2000), the idea that it is possible and necessary for the members of diverse societies to deliberate with one another in such a way as to find common solutions to political problems. Popper diverges with many of them, however, in suggesting that parties to any such dialogue must view their religious and cultural beliefs not as truth claims, but as hypotheses or conjectures, and hence, fitting subjects for debate and criticism. Critics have suggested that in requiring members of different cultural and religious groups to submit to his view as to the nature of truth, Popper's approach to negotiating a settlement between diverse cultural and religious groups causes as many problems as it solves: it is too demanding in the sense that it requires members of different groups to understand their values, and their relationship to them, in a particular and controversial way. But in this, Popper seems no less controversial or demanding than many other liberals whose work is considered central to contemporary debates. Rawls and Larmore, for example, try to establish a model of deliberative reasoning which avoids the requirement that people adopt a particular metaphysical position towards their own beliefs, only to require parties to the dialogue to present their claims in certain controversial ways, in order that they might be accepted by people with very different views about the world. Iris Marion Young's difference theory falls into a broadly similar trap, as, indeed, do the approaches defended by Parekh and Gray, all of whom, in one way or another, require members of all groups to 'talk past their differences' and engage with one another in the construction of common principles and institutions by framing their discussions in particular ways, and constraining their deliberations according to wider and prior principles which determine the rules of conduct. Popper's rejection of the 'myth' that we need to understand individuals as embedded in mutually exclusive 'frameworks' which define their identity and make it impossible for groups to deliberate with one another or come to common agreements remains powerful, insightful, and largely ignored among most political theorists, many of whom have gone on to argue for a conception of deliberative democracy very similar to that defended by Popper almost 50 years earlier (Popper, 1994a). Popper's methodological individualism – his view that the principal subject of political analysis is the individual not the groups to which they belong – and his claim that the members of different cultures, religions, and nations can (and must) come together to deliberate meaningfully with one another in order to identify and solve social and political problems regardless of their differences is indeed controversial, but no less controversial or dogmatic than many alternative approaches which are considered canonical in the literature (see Waldron, 2004).

Furthermore, just as Popper's philosophy undermines the idea that social and political reforms in the *domestic* context can be justified by an appeal to overarching historical laws, or to idealized states of affairs derived through abstract reasoning (independent of a wider system of conjectural knowledge and theory), it also suggests the folly in looking to such justifications as a basis for *international* intervention, especially in the area of democratization. In particular, it undermines the idea – dominant among Western liberal democratic states like Britain and the US – that it is possible to establish democratic regimes in societies with no history of democracy. The idea that undemocratic regimes can be swept aside and unproblematically replaced with more democratic, more enlightened political systems has been shown to be fraught with dangers, particularly in recent years. The wars in Iraq and Afghanistan, for example, are arguably a fitting testament to the kind of limits to reason (and political radicalism) that Popper described: just as it is not for politicians or philosophers in liberal democratic societies (driven by an Enlightenment faith in the power of reason) to dream up visions of the ideal society and then reform society so as to bring those visions about, so they should not consider it their role to design an ideal set of social and political institutions and then impose them upon peoples who are not ready for them, do not understand them, and have not had a hand in their shaping. Such radicalism is premised upon a blind faith in the capacity of reason to provide certainty about the kind of institutions needed, the ends to which they should be committed, and the possible pitfalls and problems which will be encountered in the process of their establishment. In fact, Popper suggested, no such certainty is possible, and to foresee all the possible variables and ramifications of individual decisions in a way that is simply not credible. Consequently, any attempts to encourage democracy in undemocratic states must necessarily be gradual, piecemeal, and the product of real dialogue among those individuals involved.

If Popper's political philosophy is too often dismissed for its historical redundancy, it is just as often dismissed for its methodological implications. Popper's ideas were as much about (if not more about) establishing the appropriate *method* for the study of political and social life as they were about producing normative or guiding principles about the structure of society and the state. They are claims about the appropriate ends of politics, and of philosophy, and hence, they articulate a particular, original, and controversial political and methodological vision. And it is not a vision which fits easily within many of the dominant approaches in contemporary political thought. It is fitting, perhaps, given Popper's epistemological commitment to falsificationism and his rejection of inductive verificationism, that it is much easier to discuss what Popper was *not* than what he *was*.

For example, Popper could not comfortably be described as a member of the 'Cambridge school' of political philosophy – embodied in the work of historians like Quentin Skinner and J. G. A. Pocock – who hold that it is the principal job of the political philosopher to derive the meaning of political texts or utterances by locating them within their particular historical context. Popper shared with historians like Skinner the claim that, when studying political and philosophical texts, there is some value in working out what the author meant to achieve by understanding the historical context in which she wrote it. That is, Popper believed that it was sometimes important to derive the 'situational logic' of a text or argument by reconstructing the historical and intentional circumstances in which it was written or uttered (Popper, 1957/2005, pp. 136–41). However, he was fiercely resistant of the more radical claim that such a process foreclosed the possibility of saying anything more meaningful about politics or society, or that political concepts, texts, or arguments could not be subjected to ahistorical analysis. Popper believed that political philosophy was more than merely the study of the language used by particular theorists at any particular moment in history and, *contra* Wittgenstein, that the point of philosophy is not merely to derive the *meaning* of linguistic or textual statements, but to determine the *truth* or *falsity* of such statements. Hence, he believed that the point of *political* philosophy is to identify social and political problems, and to resolve them. He therefore thought that it was a central aim of the social and political sciences to determine the truth or falsity of claims about social and political matters, and to work out how, and to what extent, existing social and political arrangements might be considered, or made, legitimate.

Popper was also no postmodernist. His insistence that it was possible to use the tools of reason and objectivity to reveal knowledge about all aspects of the world, from quantum mechanics to the appropriate design of social and political institutions, seems in flat contradiction to claims made by postmodernists that such an endeavour was doomed to failure. Despite going against many Enlightenment thinkers in questioning the capacity of reason to reveal certain truths about the world, he was no poststructuralist in the vein of Foucault or Bourdieu, and despite being an impassioned critic (of rival understandings of science, of authoritarianism, of totalitarianism, of many branches of philosophy), he was certainly no 'critical theorist' in the tradition of thinkers like Habermas, Adorno, or Horkheimer, for all the reasons mentioned in Chapter 3. For Popper, criticism – understood as the testing of hypotheses with counter arguments and evidence – was the primary route to genuine human knowledge, and the only real way of attaining it. Popper abhorred the moral relativism that he believed lay implicit in postmodernism, poststructuralism and critical theory, and rejected too the political impotence that he felt they implied. His aim above anything else was to provide a mechanism by which the truth and falsity of claims (about all aspects of the world, including morality) could be evaluated, and to defend the idea that individuals could, by working together, take charge of their lives and their future, and to reject the common claim among 'radical' ideologists that all that people could realistically do was wait for change to come to them.

No Cambridge historian, postmodernist, poststructuralist or critical theorist, then, Popper is perhaps most closely associated with philosophical pragmatists and the political theorists working in the Anglo-American tradition. Yet, again, he cannot be easily slotted within either of these traditions. There are numerous reasons why Popper cannot be straightforwardly labelled a member of the Anglo-American tradition, for example. Since the publication of Rawls's *A Theory of Justice* in 1971, Anglo-American political philosophy has been dominated by the search for the appropriate definition of justice and, hence, of the just society. Unlike practitioners of the Cambridge school, Rawlsian political philosophers tend not to appeal to history in their theorizing, other than in a tangential way; rather, their aim is to draw upon the analytical tradition in order to establish the rational and normative coherence of certain first principles upon which a just social and political order might be constructed. To put it another way, the principal aim of Anglo-American normative political philosophy is to derive a conception of justice substantive enough to inform the design of social and political institutions, to define these institutions' roles and responsibilities, and to circumscribe their actions, from a process of reasoned deliberation. Institutions, policies, and decisions are thus legitimated by reason (by rationally defensible arguments) rather than particular values embodied in religious, cultural, or national traditions. Consequently, Anglo-American political philosophers see themselves as engaged in the Enlightenment project of justifying the authority of political arrangements in universal standards of reason as opposed to contingent, parochial memberships or ideals. The contractualism of liberal

thinkers like Brian Barry (1995), Charles Beitz (1989), Thomas
Nagel (1991), Thomas Scanlon (1999), and John Rawls's (1971)
early work, the political liberalism of Charles Larmore (2008)
and John Rawls's (1993) later work, and the comprehensive
liberalism of thinkers like Joseph Raz (1986; 1996) and Steven
Wall (1998) all stand united with the deliberative democratic
approach defended by theorists like Amy Gutmann and Dennis
Thompson (1996), and Joshua Cohen (1989) in suggesting that
political institutions can be designed, and reforms enacted,
according to principles revealed by reasoned deliberation
among individual actors motivated to find agreement in circumstances of diversity, and that it is possible for reason (untainted
by particular values or theories) to provide a blueprint for a just
society which can be constructed from scratch. Anglo-American
liberal political philosophy thus draws inspiration from the
Enlightenment vision of thinkers like Bacon and Descartes,
who believed that the truth could be found by excising from
the mind all particularities and dispositions and looking at the
world through clean eyes.

Popper, of course, agreed that political authority should be
justified by reason rather than particularist identities or values,
but he had little time for the Baconian or Cartesian vision of
reasoning upon which the Anglo-American normative project
appears to be built, believing it irresponsible, arrogant, and
contrary to the growth of knowledge. He did not share Rawls's
belief that the aim of political philosophy should be the deri-
vation of principles of justice which could be used to structure
and regulate social and political institutions. Such a project was,
Popper thought, indicative of the blind optimism among many
Enlightenment thinkers in the power of reason to sweep aside
history and to construct fully functioning social and political
systems as if the past had never existed. Rawls and many of his
followers are, in Popper's terms, merely the contemporary
advocates of the same mistaken epistemology as the French
revolutionaries. Consequently, they fall into the same trap: their
attempts to describe a functioning and just society will inevitably

and necessarily be thwarted by the conjectural character of what passes for all knowledge, and the inability of reason to foresee all possible variables and, hence, to deal with all possible challenges. Rawlsian theories of social justice tend to be demanding and substantive – they stipulate how the benefits and burdens of society should be redistributed, for example, as well as what these benefits and burdens are. Popper's fallibilism about the power of abstract reasoning to resolve these questions once and for all, and his attendant scepticism about long-term centralized planning, provides an important check on the aspirations of many philosophers working in the Anglo-American tradition to settle the question of justice in the way that they do, and suggests that they should view their claims about justice in more humble terms than they sometimes do, as hypotheses and suggestions, rather than rationally verifiable truths.

Similarly, Popper would have had little time for the idea that the central aim of political philosophy was to define the meaning of terms like 'justice'. Hence, he would have considered the tendency among many Anglo-American philosophers to frame questions in terms of the definition of essences (such as 'what is justice?', or 'what is equality?'), that currently dominates contemporary Anglo-American political philosophy, as a redundant and futile activity. Popper was primarily interested in identifying and solving problems in a context in which it was impossible to provide ultimate and final definitions of such terms as equality, justice, or liberty, and in which we should be sceptical of leaders or intellectuals who seek to provide such things. In particular, he was interested in the power of, and limits to, knowledge, and hence, the justification that rulers might appropriately give for enacting social reforms. Given this, it is hardly surprising that Popper remains such a marginal figure in mainstream normative discourse. After all, if his epistemological claims are correct (and it is not possible for reason to reveal certain truths about the world), and if it is also true that philosophy should not concern itself with the definition of terms like justice, equality, or freedom, then an important concern of normative political

philosophers working in the Anglo-American tradition is rendered little more than a pointless mistake. They appeal to a
mistaken conception of Enlightenment reasoning in order to
produce ideal definitions of political terms which are unhelpful
because their coherence or persuasiveness cannot be proven.

Despite all this, there are a number of ways in which Popper's
ideas are more congruent with those of Anglo-American political theorists than we might first think, and more than many
thinkers within this tradition assume. For example, many if not
all philosophers working in the Rawlsian tradition would agree
with Popper that it is the principal role of the political philosopher to identify and seek to resolve genuine social and political
problems. For example, while liberal political philosophers like
Ronald Dworkin seek to answer questions like 'what is equality?',
it is clear that they do so primarily in order to identify and resolve
real social and political problems: liberal egalitarians of various
stripes are principally motivated by the theoretical and practical
question of how social and political institutions might measure
and ameliorate unjust economic inequalities (e.g. Cohen, 2008;
Dworkin, 2000). Multiculturalist liberals and political liberals
are concerned, among other things, with resolving the question
of how broadly impartial liberal democratic institutions might
appropriately take into account the diverse interests of cultural,
ethnic, and religious minorities (e.g. Kymlicka, 1997; Raz, 1996).
And the increasing number of political philosophers working
in the area of international justice generally seek answers to
complex practical questions including the alleviation of poverty
and suffering among the world's poor (e.g. Pogge, 2007). The
point for these thinkers, then, is not to engage in abstract
reasoning for the sake of it, but to apply the tools of what
Popper called the rationalist tradition to concrete social and
political problems in the world in a clear-headed, analytical way,
in order that such problems might be resolved. Their defini-
tional questions are therefore discussed in the context of, and
in response to, the actually existing nature of these problems.
Popper would emphasize the conjectural, hypothetical nature

of any such resolutions, of course; he would indeed claim that reasoning needs to be conducted against the background of accumulated knowledge, and he would also point out that the answers provided should not be considered certain truths, but there is no reason to suppose that Anglo-American normative political philosophers could not unite with Popper on the idea that political philosophy (like any other discipline) is at heart a process of problem-solving, and that reason can provide the solutions to concrete social, political, economic, and legal problems.

Popper also shared with many contemporary Anglo-American political philosophers a rejection of teleological morality: that is, the idea that it is appropriate to determine the moral rightness or wrongness of an act or set of institutions according to the extent to which this act or set of institutions is in line with, or helps to bring about, some pre-determined conception of the good life for all. The majority of contemporary liberal egalitarians, libertarians, classical liberals, political liberals, and comprehensive liberals have united behind the claim (made by H. L. A Hart in his *A Concept of Law,* and, differently, by Rawls in his *A Theory of Justice*), that utilitarian teleology is *morally* deficient as it can lead to injustices like the oppression of minority groups, and have also joined Rawls in defending a broadly 'deontological' form of liberalism in its place. Popper's political philosophy strengthens the liberal case against teleological moral and political systems by providing a different, and perhaps even more powerful, *epistemological* critique of its core assumptions: that any moral theory which evaluates the rightness or wrongness of an act or decision according to the extent to which it brings about some future overarching good for all is not only morally inadequate but epistemologically incoherent, for no such overarching good can be known. Similarly, Popper's argument serves to undermine certain more radical varieties of moral consequentialism: any moral theory which evaluates the rightness or the wrongness of an act or decision according to the consequences it would have is undermined by the fact that

(a) in order to know whether the resultant consequences are good or bad requires a prior knowledge of the goals to which they should be aimed (which is possible, but difficult, given the fallibility of reason), and (b) because the consequences – especially the long-term consequences – of any such act or decision cannot be known with certainty. This, we must remember, was the reason that Popper was committed to what he called a 'negative' rather than a 'positive' utilitarianism. He believed that we can and should seek to identify problems in society and propose solutions to them which bring about beneficial consequences, but we should not seek to construct over-arching conceptions of the good life and judge actions right or wrong depending on the extent to which they bring about this conception of the good life. The consequences of our actions are thus important in our moral deliberations, but state action can only be coherently employed in the interests of *reducing harm* rather than *promoting a particular political vision*.

Finally, there is one further, much more fundamental, claim which unites Popper with contemporary political theorists working in the Anglo-American tradition, namely, that normative statements about politics and society are both meaningful and possible. Remember, at the time at which Popper was writing, analytical philosophy was dominated by the logical positivism of the Vienna Circle, and the ordinary language philosophy of thinkers like Austin and Ryle. Together, these dominating forces appeared to foreclose entirely the idea that it is possible to make normative statements about such things as politics or society or morality. After all, logical positivists held that such statements were meaningless and, hence, could not be described as philosophical statements at all. And ordinary language philosophers suggested that the meaning of political concepts (and, hence, the normative justification of statements about political or social life) could not be separated from the context in which they were used: in asking the question 'what is freedom?', for example, ordinary language philosophers suggested that what we are really asking is 'in what ways do individuals in a particular context use the word "freedom"'? Such an approach appeared to rule out any attempt to provide universal definitions of such terms and, hence, meant that normative discussions about their importance (and how they might be protected or encouraged) could represent nothing more or less than a general conversation about the various meanings of the terms in question.

The dominance of logical positivism and ordinary language philosophy, and their foreclosure of normativity, led numerous thinkers like Isaiah Berlin and Peter Laslett to worry that political theory was dead (Berlin, 1962; Laslett, 1956). Popper may not have single-handedly destroyed logical positivism and ordinary language theory in quite the way he claimed to have, but he was nevertheless instrumental in breaking their grip on philosophy and making room for normativity *within* a philosophical approach informed by analytical rigour. Popper's rejection of the inductive scientific model, and his claim that science should be concerned with the falsification of conjectural statements about the world rather than the inductive extrapolation of general laws, suggested that philosophy could (and should) adopt a 'scientific' method, but that doing so did not foreclose the possibility of normative statements or deny the philosophical status of statements about politics, society, ethics, or metaphysics. Popper's epistemology provided a (controversial) way of rendering metaphysical, political, and ethical statements (and hence, normativity) compatible with the kind of rigour and clarity of purpose which defined the analytical tradition. Although his influence is often overlooked, therefore, it is nevertheless fair to suggest that Popper's work was instrumental in establishing the philosophical conditions in which other thinkers (like H. L. A. Hart and John Rawls) would produce their most notable normative works.

Furthermore, in reasserting political philosophy as the search for solutions to concrete social and political problems, rather than the quest for ultimate truths or essences, Popper helped prepare the way for pragmatists like Richard Rorty (e.g. 1989) to

argue for the rejection of foundationalism in political philosophy, and for Anglo-American political theorists working in
the Rawlsian tradition to make normative claims independently
of any wider account of truth. In Rorty, for example, we find the
Popperian claim that philosophers should not concern themselves with determining certain truths, as such truths cannot
not be reliably known, and that they should, instead, seek to
solve concrete political problems in the world using the historical, analytical, and philosophical tools currently at their disposal.
The search for truth is not only pointless, Rorty thought, but
pointlessly diverting: philosophers who seek ultimate truths
will inevitably spend so much time looking for them that they
will have little or no time to address the real and enduring problems faced by real people living in the world. Like Popper,
then, Rortean pragmatists rejected the idea that in order to
discuss philosophical ideas, we first have to derive the philosophical foundations (or essences) of these ideas and, like
Popper, they argued that social and political problems can be
resolved through the collective deliberations of individual actors.
As Rorty argued, the real project for political philosophers is
not to find ultimate and final *truths*, but to find coherent *justifications* for the claims we make about the world and politics.
Popper, like Rorty, believed that it was possible to gain knowledge of the world, and of the ideas we use to describe and make
sense of it, without first revealing their essences or, in Rorty's
words, the foundations upon which these ideas rest. Hence, for
Popper and for Rorty, the principal goal of political philosophy
was to find grounds for political principles in the absence of
firm foundations or clearly determined essences. Consequently,
pragmatists, like Popper, asserted the importance of collective
deliberation and agreement among individual actors who
possess limited information but who are motivated to find
agreeable solutions to common problems.

And this, it must be said, is a goal that is now shared not only
by pragmatists but by the vast majority of political theorists
working in the Anglo-American tradition. A growing number of

Anglo-American political philosophers now share with the pragmatists and with Popper the claim that it is not the point of political philosophy to reveal certain truths about the world, but to seek justification for common political principles in circumstances in which there is profound, and perhaps insoluble, disagreement regarding questions of truth. Earlier in this chapter I mentioned the rise of multiculturalism as a political and philosophical issue, and mentioned some of the ways in which contemporary political theorists have tried to deal with this issue. Common to all of them, and to political liberals like Rawls in particular, is the idea that we live in a world characterised by radical disagreement about such fundamental matters as the origins of life, the nature of humanity, and our place in the world. We live in a world of different religions and moral perspectives, many of which are incompatible with one another, but which are nevertheless held to be incredibly important by hundreds of millions of people throughout the world. Given this, any conception of political philosophy which takes as its principal goal the settling of questions about truth, and which seeks to justify social and political arrangements and policies in these accounts of truth will inevitably fail or, at least, will remain inconclusive and partial, and unacceptable to many people. Political philosophy cannot, and should not try to, resolve questions of truth, and *liberal* political philosophers in particular should not attempt to do so, as such things are, for liberals, rightly left to individual conscience. The principal question for most Anglo-American political philosophers working today is not, arguably, what constitutes truth, but how we might derive political principles, institutions, and policies which are fair in the sense that they might be found acceptable by all those who live under them, irrespective of their more fundamental ideas about the world. This is a project that Popper believed in, and to which he made important contributions. The point of political philosophy for Popper, as wells as for pragmatists like Rorty, political liberals like Rawls, difference theorists like Young, deliberative democrats like Gutmann, and many

other contemporary Anglo-American political philosophers is
not to uncover the truth in order that it might provide some
unifying moral basis for political authority, or for some particular arrangement of social and political institutions or some set
of policies, but to build an inclusive political system in the face
of radical disagreement about what is true about the world.

Popper cannot be easily associated with the Cambridge school,
then, nor postmodernism, poststructuralism, or critical theory.
He did not occupy the same theoretical space as Rawls or his
followers, although his conclusions hold an enduring relevance
in the areas in which they work. He was not a utilitarian in the
way many understand the term, nor a teleologist, although he
was committed to evaluating the success or failure of proposed
social reforms at least partly in response to the consequences
they generated. He was not a relativist, a nationalist, or a com-
munitarian, but recognized the important (and often pernicious) hold that particularist memberships have had over so many
people throughout history. He was not strictly a conservative,
nor a libertarian, nor a classical liberal, but rejected long-term
social, economic, and political planning and influenced many
who associate themselves with those traditions. He was not a
socialist, but he believed that state institutions can and should
alleviate the crippling poverty that he believed many people
endured. He was briefly a Marxist, and throughout his life continued to respect Marx's contribution to economic and social
thought, but ultimately saw him as a danger to the aims of the
open society. He supported the ideals embodied in the Enlightenment while fiercely criticizing many Enlightenment thinkers,
defended a politics based on reason while asserting its limits,
and championed the growth of knowledge while claiming that
certain knowledge was impossible. In *The Open Society* he presented an important statement of post-war social democracy,
rooted in an epistemology which would be used by many to
destroy it. He was not a social contract thinker like Locke,
Hobbes, Rousseau, or Kant. He did not rest his conclusions
on controversial claims about human nature or the content of

human motivations. He did not concern himself explicitly with many of the questions which political theorists take to be of core importance in the discipline, like political obligation, rights, and the source of law. And he did not provide a full and thoroughgoing normative theory of politics. Many philosophers vehemently disagreed with Popper's epistemological, social, and political philosophy, and consequently dismissed his work as mistaken, based upon faulty reasoning, or slipshod scholarship. Also, there are indeed important issues about which Popper said little or nothing, and which his philosophy does not seem equipped to tackle. It is hardly surprising, then, that the overwhelming majority of contemporary political philosophers, political scientists, economists, social theorists, and sociologists do not really know what to do with Popper, and it is hardly surprising that they have decided not to do anything with him. Popper was a polymath and a contrarian. He wrote on so many subjects, and excited controversy in so many fields, that it is possible for everyone to find something in his work to disagree profoundly with. The contradictions in his work, his forthright, often polemical written style, and his dogged commitment to principles which he thought were right in the face of what he called passing fads and trends make him difficult to locate in the literature, and hence he is, and remains, a marginal figure in contemporary political philosophy.

Conclusion

Popper belongs to a select group of thinkers whose name can be used as an adjective to describe theories and approaches (statements may be described as Popperian, or Wittgensteinian, or Rawlsian, for example). But there is no Popper*ism*, as there is Marxism or Platonism – no substantive ideology or normative programme around which supporters can rally. This is only to be expected, of course. Popper's rejection of historicism, his commitment to experimentation, piecemeal social reform, and the uncertainty of human knowledge meant that his work did not lend itself to the kind of world building (or destroying) that ideologies inspire. Indeed, in so far as ideologies represent sets of truth claims about the ideal ends of social and political institutions, they are, on Popper's terms, at best inherently fragile and partial. At worst, they embody the mistaken desire among their supporters to predict the future course of human development towards some ideal state of affairs – a desire which Popper saw as legitimating tyranny.

Popper did not leave us with an ideology, then. What he gave us was a method for finding out what we can and cannot know about the world and ourselves; a means of testing and evaluating the claims made by those who would rule us or seek to tell us how to live. He did not give us a list of policies to enact, or an institutional blueprint to establish. Indeed, he argued that the desire among many political philosophers and activists to provide such a thing is precisely the problem that we need to avoid. Rather, he provided a way of finding out what the appropriate policies and institutions might be, and how they might be justified. And in doing so, he provided a vision of politics and society which embraced individual freedom, equality, and reason. Popper believed that whatever their particular nature, social and political institutions should be structured in ways which encourage freedom of thought and discussion, and which protect individuals from tyranny; the tyranny of leaders who assume to know what is best for humankind, from institutions which fail to check the power of these leaders, and from domination by the 'economically strong' who are able to wield their economic power to subjugate and manipulate those who have less or nothing. He believed in the power of all individuals to seek common agreement on solutions to social and political matters through reasonable argument and empathy, and hence, fervently believed in democracy. He believed in the unifying character of reason, and that reason (appropriately understood) provided the key to breaking down the mentality of 'us' and 'them', characteristic of the closed society, and encouraging a universal concern for all human beings throughout the world, wherever they may live. His politics was consequently defined by what we might call a cosmopolitan rationalism – the idea that all people in all nations should receive help if they so need it, and that all people throughout the world might engage in productive dialogue with one another about political and social problems. He believed in the open society; a political community characterized by free thought and discussion; by democratic institutions accountable to those under them; by a spirit of cooperation not merely with one's neighbours, but with all persons for whom knowledge, experimentation, truth, freedom, and equality are important virtues; and by a rejection of all those pernicious ideas of historical fate, of common destiny, of nation, and of irrationalism which have provided leaders through the ages with the philosophical tools they need to rob individuals of their freedom, to manipulate them, to divide them, and, ultimately, to kill them. He believed in the capacity of individuals to bring about real and genuine change but recognized the need for change to be gradual rather than radical, incremental rather than revolutionary. In politics as in science, Popper believed that truth emerges out of the clash of ideas. Even the most sacred of cows, the most perfect and beautiful of theories, must be forced to prove themselves against rival theories; no theory is beyond criticism, and indeed, should it ever be conceived to be, the theory would lose its explanatory power. Just as Newton's claims about physics could not claim unassailable validity, so the theories of political thinkers and ideologues should also fall under the critical gaze of those who would seek to falsify them. Popper's methodological work in the field of epistemology, when applied to society and politics, provided a genuinely innovative approach to understanding the aims of philosophy and the state, and at once provided a new perspective on the debate about the possibility of a 'social science'. Such a thing was indeed possible, he believed, but establishing it would require an entirely new understanding of science.

Bibliography

Adorno, T. W. (1973) *Negative Dialectics*. London: Routledge. (First published in German, 1963).

Adorno, T. W., H. Albert, R. Dahrendorf, J. Habermas, H. Pilot, & K. Popper (eds.) (1976) *The Positivist Dispute in German Sociology*. New York: Harper. (First published in German, 1969).

Agassi, J. (1993) *A Philosopher's Apprentice: In Karl Popper's Workshop (Series in the Philosophy of Karl R. Popper and Critical Rationalism*. Atlanta, GA: Editions Rodopi.

Arendt, H. (1951/2004) *The Origins of Totalitarianism*. Orlando, FL: Schocken Books.

Aron, R. (1957) *The Opium of the Intellectuals*. New York: Doubleday

Banbrough, R. (ed.) (1967) *Plato, Popper, and Politics: Some Contributions to a Modern Controversy*. Cambridge: W. Heffer & Sons.

Barry, B. (1995) *Justice as Impartiality: A Treatise on Social Justice, Vol. 2*. Oxford: Clarendon Press.

Beitz, C. (1989) *Political Equality*. Princeton, NJ: Princeton University Press.

Benhabib, S. (1992) *Situating the Self: Gender, Community, and Postmodernism in Contemporary Ethics*. London: Routledge.

Berlin, I. (1962) 'Does Political Theory Exist?' in P. Laslett & W. G. Runciman (eds) *Philosophy, Politics, and Society* (pp. 1–33). Series 2, Oxford: Blackwell.

Bevir, M. (1999) *The Logic of the History of Ideas*. Cambridge: Cambridge University Press.

Blundell, J. (1999) 'Introduction' in *The Road to Serfdom: The Condensed Edition* (pp. 14–24). London: Institute of Economic Affairs.

Burke, E. (1790/1986) *Reflections on the Revolution in France*. London: Penguin.

Brzezinski, Z. (1956) *The Permanent Purge: Politics in Soviet Totalitarianism*. Cambridge, MA: Harvard University Press.

Catton, P. & G. MacDonald (eds) (2004) *Karl Popper: Critical Appraisals*. London: Routledge.

Cohen, G. A. (2008) *Rescuing Justice and Equality*. Cambridge, MA: Harvard University Press.

Cohen, J. (1989) 'Deliberation and Democratic Legitimacy' in Alan Hamlin and Phillip Petit (eds) *The Good Polity* (pp. 17–34.). Cambridge, MA: Blackwell.

Cornforth, M. (1968) *The Open Philosophy and the Open Society: A Reply to Sir Karl Popper's Refutations of Marxism.* London: Lawrence & Wishart.

Crossman, R. H. S. (1959) *Plato Today.* 2nd edition. London: George Allen & Unwin.

Derrida, J. (1967) *Of Grammatology.* Baltimore, MD: Johns Hopkins University Press. (Originally published in French, 1967).

Duhem, P. (1954) *The Aim and Structure of Physical Theory.* Princeton, NJ: Princeton University Press.

Dworkin, R. (2000) *Sovereign Virtue: The Theory and Practice of Equality.* Cambridge, MA: Harvard University Press.

Edmonds, D. & J. Eidenow (2002) *Wittgenstein's Poker: The Story of a Ten Minute Argument Between Two Great Philosophers.* London: Faber.

Feyerabend, P. (1975/1993) *Against Method: Outline of an Anarchistic Theory of Knowledge.* London: Verso.

Fite, W. (1934) *The Platonic Legend.* New York: C. Scribner's Sons.

Fraser, N. (1997) *Justice Interruptus: Critical Reflections on the Post-Socialist Condition.* New York: Routledge.

Gamble, A. (1996) *Hayek: The Iron Cage of Liberty.* Cambridge: Polity Press.

Geuss, R. (1981) *The Idea of a Critical Theory: Habermas & the Frankfurt School.* Cambridge: Cambridge University Press.

Gray, J. (2000) *Two Faces of Liberalism.* Cambridge: Polity Press.

Gutmann, A. & D. Thompson (1996) *Democracy & Disagreement.* Cambridge: Cambridge University Press.

Habermas, J. (1971) *Knowledge and Human Interests.* Boston, MA: Beacon Press.

Habermas, J. (1976) 'A Positively Bisected Rationalism' in T. W. Adorno, H. Albert, R. Dahrendorf, J. Habermas, H. Pilot, & K. Popper (eds) *The Positivist Dispute in German Sociology* (pp. 198–225). New York: Harper and Row.

Habermas, J. (1989) *The Structural Transformation of the Public Sphere: An Inquiry into a Category of Bourgeois Society.* Cambridge: Polity Press. (Originally published in German, 1962).

Hacohen, M. (2000) *Karl Popper: The Formative Years, 1902 – 1945: Politics and Philosophy in Interwar Vienna.* Cambridge: Cambridge University Press.

Hart, H. L. A. (1961/1997) *The Concept of Law.* Oxford: Oxford University Press.

Hayek, F. A. (1944) *The Road to Serfdom*. London: Routledge.

Hayek, F. A. (1960) *The Constitution of Liberty*. London: Routledge.

Hirschmann, N. (2003) *The Subject of Liberty: Toward a Feminist Theory of Freedom*. Princeton, NJ: Princeton University Press.

Horkheimer, M. (1997) *Dialectic of Enlightenment*. Revised edition. London: Verso. (Originally published in German, 1944).

Hume, D. (1748/2008) *An Enquiry into Human Understanding*. Oxford: Oxford Classics.

Jarvie, I. C. & S. Pralong (1999) *Popper's Open Society After 50 Years: The Continuing Relevance of Karl Popper*. London: Routledge.

Jarvie, I. C., K. Milford, & D. Miller (2006) *Karl Popper: A Centenary Assessment*. Aldershot: Ashgate.

Kauffman, W. (1959) *From Shakespeare to Existentialism: Studies in Poetry, Religion, and Philosophy*. Boston, MA: Beacon Press.

Kuhn, T. S. (1962) *The Structure of Scientific Revolutions*. Chicago, IL: University of Chicago Press.

Kymlicka, W. (1997) *Multicultural Citizenship: A Liberal Theory of Minority Rights*. Oxford: Clarendon Press.

Lakatos, I. (1976) *Proofs and Refutations*. Cambridge: Cambridge University Press.

Lakatos, I. (1978a) *The Methodology of Scientific Research Programmes: Philosophical Papers Vol. 1*. Cambridge: Cambridge University Press.

Lakatos, I. (1978b) *Mathematics, Science, and Epistemology: Philosophical Papers Vol. 2*. Cambridge: Cambridge University Press.

Lane, M. (2001) *Plato's Progeny: How Socrates and Plato Still Captivate the Modern Mind*. London: Duckworth.

Larmore, C. (2008) *The Autonomy of Morality*. Cambridge: Cambridge University Press.

Laslett, P. (1956) 'Introduction' in P. Laslett (ed.) *Philosophy, Politics, and Society*. Series 1, Oxford: Blackwell.

Levinson, P. (ed.) (1982) *In Pursuit of Truth: Essays on the Philosophy of Karl Popper on the Occasion of his 80th Birthday*. Atlantic Highlands, NJ: Humanities Press.

Levinson, R. B. (1953) *In Defence of Plato*. Cambridge, MA: Harvard University Press.

MacIntyre, A. (1996) *After Virtue: A Study in Moral Theory*. London: Duckworth.

Magee, B. (1973) *Karl Popper*. London: Penguin.

Mandeville, B. (1714/1988) *The Fable of the Bees: or, Private Vices, Public Benefits*. Indianapolis: Liberty Fund.

Marcuse, H. (1964) *One Dimensional Man: Studies in the Ideology of Advanced Industrial Society*. Boston, MA: Beacon Press.

Marx, K. (1932/1988) *Economic and Philosophic Manuscripts of 1844*. New York: Prometheus Books.

Menger, C. (1871/1981) *Principles of Economics*. New York: New York University Press.

Miller, D. (1994) *Critical Rationalism: A Restatement and Defence*. Chicago, IL: Open Court Publishing Company.

Miller, D. (1995) *On Nationality*. Oxford: Clarendon Press.

Mises, L. von, (1922/1951) *Socialism: An Economic and Social Analysis*. New Haven, CT: Yale University Press.

Mises, L. von, (1949) *Human Action: A Treatise on Economics*. New Haven, CT: Yale University Press.

Munz, P. (1985) *Our Knowledge of the Growth of Knowledge*. London: Routledge.

Nagel, T. (1991) *Equality and Partiality*. New York: Oxford University Press.

Nozick, R. (1974) *Anarchy, State, and Utopia*. New York: Basic Books.

O'Hear, A. (1980) *Karl Popper*. London: Routledge.

O'Hear, A. (ed.) (2004) *Karl Popper: Critical Assessments of Leading Philosophers*. 4 Vols. London: Routledge.

Parekh, B. (2005) *Re-Thinking Multiculturalism: Cultural Diversity and Political Theory*. 2nd edition. Basingstoke: Palgrave Macmillan.

Plamenatz, J. (1952/1967) 'The Open Society and Its Enemies,' *The British Journal of Sociology 3*. 264–73. Reprinted in R. Banbrough (ed.) (1967) *Plato, Popper, and Politics: Some Contributions to a Modern Controversy*. Cambridge: W. Heffer & Sons.

Pogge, T. W. (2007) *World Poverty and Human Rights*. Cambridge: Polity Press.

Polanyi, K. (1944/2001) *The Great Transformation: The Political and Economic Origins of Our Times*. Boston, MA: Beacon Press.

Popper, K. (1935/2007a) *The Logic of Scientific Discovery*. London: Routledge.

Popper, K. (1945/2006a) *The Open Society and Its Enemies 1: The Spell of Plato*. London: Routledge.

Popper, K. (1945/2006b) *The Open Society and Its Enemies 2: Hegel and Marx*. London: Routledge.

Popper, K. (1957/2005) *The Poverty of Historicism*. London: Routledge.

Popper, K. (1963/2007b) *Conjectures and Refutations: The Growth of Scientific Knowledge*. London: Routledge.

Popper, K. (1972/1979) *Objective Knowledge: An Evolutionary Approach*. Oxford: Oxford University Press.

Popper, K. (1974/2002) *Unended Quest: An Intellectual Autobiography*. London: Routledge.

Popper, K. (1977/2003a) *The Self and Its Brain: An Argument for Interactionism.* London: Routledge. With Sir John C. Eccles.

Popper, K. (1984/2000) *In Search of a Better World: Lectures and Essays from Thirty Years.* London: Routledge.

Popper, K. (1994a) *The Myth of the Framework: In Defence of Science and Rationality.* London: Routledge. Edited by M. A. Notturno.

Popper, K. (1994b) *Knowledge and the Mind-Body Problem: In Defence of Interactionism,* London: Routledge. Edited by M. A. Notturno.

Popper, K. (1994/2003b) *All Life is Problem Solving.* London: Routledge.

Popper, K. (2008) *After the Open Society: Selected Social and Political Writings.* London: Routledge. Edited by J. Shearmur & P. N. Turner.

Putnam, H. (1974). 'The "corroboration" of theories', in P. A. Schilpp (ed.) *The Philosophy of Karl Popper* (pp. 221–40). LaSalle, IL: Open Court.

Quine, W. V. O. (1960) *Word and Object.* Cambridge, MA: MIT Press.

Rand, A. (1943) *The Fountainhead.* Indiana, IN: Bobbs-Merrill Company.

Rawls, J. (1971) *A Theory of Justice.* Oxford: Oxford University Press.

Rawls, J. (1993) *Political Liberalism.* New York: Columbia University Press.

Raz, J. (1986) *The Morality of Freedom.* Oxford: Clarendon Press.

Raz, J. (1996) *Ethics in the Public Domain: Essays in the Morality of Law and Politics.* Oxford: Clarendon Press.

Rorty, R. (1989) *Contingency, Irony, and Solidarity.* Cambridge: Cambridge University Press.

Sandel, M. (1982) *Liberalism and the Limits of Justice.* Cambridge: Cambridge University Press.

Scanlon, T. M. (1999) *What We Owe To Each Other.* Cambridge, MA: Harvard University Press.

Schmitt, C. (1923/1988) *The Crisis of Parliamentary Democracy.* Boston, MA: MIT Press.

Schmitt, C. (1927/2006) *The Concept of the Political.* Chicago, IL: Chicago University Press.

Shearmur, J. (1996) *The Political Thought of Karl Popper.* London: Routledge.

Smith, A. (1789/2002) *The Theory of the Moral Sentiments.* Cambridge: Cambridge University Press.

Stokes, G. (1998) *Popper: Philosophy, Politics and Scientific Method.* Cambridge: Polity Press.

Tamir, Y. (1993) *Liberal Nationalism.* Princeton, NJ: Princeton University Press.

Taylor, C. (1958) 'The Poverty of the Poverty of Historicism,' *Universities and Left Review 4.* 77–78.

Waldron, J. (2004) 'Tribalism and the Myth of the Framework: Some Popperian Thoughts on the Politics of Cultural Recognition,' in P. Catton & G. MacDonald (eds) *Karl Popper: Critical Appraisals* (pp. 203–30). London: Routledge.

Wall, S. (1998) *Liberalism, Perfectionism, and Restraint.* Cambridge: Cambridge University Press.

Watkins, J. (1984) *Science and Scepticism.* Princeton, NJ: Princeton University Press, 1984.

Weimer, W. & D. Palermo (1982) *Cognition and the Symbolic Processes.* Vol. 2. Hillsdale, NJ: Lawrence Erlbaum Associates.

Wild, J. (1953) *Plato's Modern Enemies and the Theory of Natural Law.* Chicago, IL: University of Chicago Press.

Winspear, A. D. (1940) *The Genesis of Plato's Thought.* New York: S. A. Russell.

Young, I. M. (1990) *Justice and the Politics of Difference.* Princeton, NJ: Princeton University Press.

Young I. M. (2000) *Inclusion and Democracy.* Oxford: Clarendon Press.

Index

Vienna Circle, The 12–19, 25,
42, 43, 119, 144
defence of logical positivism 13
see also logical positivism
dissolution of 19–21
members of 13
Popper's critique of 16–18,
33
Popper's exclusion from 12–13
and Wittgenstein 17–18
Vienna Fabian Society 4

Waissman, Friedrich 13, 21
Waldron, Jeremy 29
Wall, Steven 140
Watkins, John 96
Wild, John 99

William, Frederick, of Prussia 99
Wittgenstein, Ludwig 12, 26
analytical and synthetic
statements 14–15
and the demarcation of physics
and metaphysics 14
see also logical positivism
and language 14–15, 17–18,
45, 138
and meaningfulness 14–15
and observation 14
Popper's attitude towards
17–18, 26
on the scope of philosophy 15,
17–18, 23, 26

Young, Iris Marion 116, 134, 147